PREDICTION FUTURE OIL MARKET NEED CHANGE

JOHN LOK

Made with ♥ on the Notion Press Platform
www.notionpress.com

Contents

Preface

The intersection of behavioral economics, energy economics, and national resource strategy provides a unique framework for evaluating how the United States manages its consumption of oil, gas, and natural resources.

In the context of economic literature and behavioral market analysis—such as the frameworks explored by my opinion research on economic theories and market behavior—resource demand is driven not merely by classical supply and demand curves, but by complex psychological factors, organizational behaviors, and systemic societal requirements.

Prologue

Table of content

Price and regulatory policies factor incentivises less energy need to transport and influences oil price reduces and oil demand reduces

Non -manual driving vehicle influences oil need to vehicle reduces and oil price decrease
What factors influence amount of energy that a networked economy ?
Oil manufacturing raising cost influences oil price rises
Household energy use: Applying behavioural economics to understand engery consumer decision-making and energy useful behaviour.

The elasticity of oil production and consumption influences energy consumer useful behavior

Climate Pollution Change how infleunces on Our
Energy need reduces

CHAPTER ONE

Why human needs to consider oil possible shortage

Gas/oil is one kind of important energy to provide to our daily lives, because any public transport tools, e.g. airplanes, ships, buses, taxis, ferries, trains, trams, etc. they must need gas / oil / electricity energy to have power to move on the roads, on the seas or on the sky. IN our houses, we also need oil to cook any foods. Oil can also be changed to be electricity energy to provide power to television, radio, light to turn on at our homes. When we have needs to watch television, listen music, read books at homes. Even, any public buildings, e.g. offices, private tall properties public facilities also need electricity to provide power, e.g. lifts. It needs electricity energy to provide power to move in order to catch anyone go to any floors in short time rapidly. Hence, it seems that global economic activities as well as our daily lives activities will be brought negative influence if one day, our earth can not provide gas to supply to any countries to use immediately. So, when one day has without gas/oil/electricity supply to our earth to use, it will bring global economic activities can not carried out, then we shall bring serious high economic loss. I assumes that how our global economic loss will be influenced if oil can not be provided to global businessmen as well as householders to live in one month, even more than one month. Hence, we can not neglect how to reduce oil shortage problem won't be occurred in our future days.

In fact, oil source or element is came from animals, when they die, their bodies will be useful element to be manufactured to oil or gas energy product when their bodied are sunk into any lands and forests or oceans in natural longing time keeping environment. SO, it seems that animals' natural death and their bodies must be any kinds of oil important elements source. SO,human must bot neglect to consider how to keep any kinds of animals' bodies to be kept into any lands or oceans long time in order to let oil scientists may research any death animals bodies elements form oceans or lands easily, such as oil refining lands , because any kinds of animals' bodies are the essential elements to let us to manufacture any kinds of gas, oil, even electricity energy. So, it beings this question: How can we keep or create oil energy?

IN fact, various energy sources exist does not mean that they are easy to get or they can provide enough reliable, affordable energy for the global population. More than 1.2 billion people would wide still lack access to electricity, and more than 2.5 billion still use wood, charcoal, and dung for the energy to cook and heat. The fact, that demand is this much greater than supply makes energy a prime market for growth. As those billions of people in Africa, Asia and South America begin to need the comfort of the developed world. Moreover, energy like all other investments, carries risks, policy is always changing. Improved technology can quickly make technology obsolete. Moreover, if you identify and properly manage the risks, energy can provide above average returns that many other sectors can not.

IN earliest days, humankind relied solely on muscular and biomass sources of energy. People needed to huel only themselves. Their animals and their fires. Water and wind is the earliest energy to provide people to sail ships around globe. Then, electricity is its known today began with MIchael Faraday's generation invention of the electric motor in 1821.

So, electricity energy is the earliest energy invention. Then, the perfection of the internal combustion engine provided the fuel dermand that has sustained the oil industry to this day, used for thousands of years by many civilizations because of its medicinal and sealing properties, oil began to be used as an energy source for lamps. But, the real advanced did not came
until centuries later, when petrolem was first fractionated at Yale university in 1954, and the ability to refine fuels from oil spread around the world. The first modern refinery was built at the pechelbronn oil field in 1857. A field that was active until 1970 and was the pechelbronn of oil service companies like Schumberger (NYSE, SCB) and Amtar, now a unit of
UGI Corporation (NYSW: UGI).

However, gas is a key to think of energy as simply fuel for car and electricity for your home. Energy is found in every product to buy, own and use. Companies do not just use energy to transport goods from production sites to retail sites, that use it to make products themselves, e.g. constructing the average car requires up to 1,700 gallons of oil, making the average
computer requires more than ten times its weight in fossil fuels, every calorie of food eaten in U.S. requires roughly ten calories of fossil fuels. For householders, you also spend electricity energy of natural gas you consume relative to daily lives. You should also notice the growing use of electric vehicles in response to raising oil prices. This is a logical , market -based reaction to continually high oil and gas prices.

Hence, for investment purposes, each source of energy is considered its own market sector. Fossil fuels, non-renewable energy consumption , with a 92 percent market share, renewable fuels like hydroelectricity, solar , wind and biofuels accounts for one -third of global energy consumption. This includes crude oil, shale oil, oil sands and liquid content of natural gas, called natural gas liquid or NGLs. As a result , of including these different forms, you sometimes see different numbers depending on the source and whether its reporting just crude oil or total liquids. Nowadays, oil is traded by the barrel, which contain 42 gallons. The common unit used for oil is thousand barrels per day. Abbreviated t b/d. Hence, it seems that oil is still the main energy source to be our essential main energy need product.

According to the international Energy Agency's (IEA's) world energy outlook 2012, global energy demand will grow more than 33% through 2035, with China, India, and Middle East accounting for 60% of the increase . Demand in developed nations will rise only marginally, with a noticeable shift away from oil and coal and toward low-carbon sources like natural gas and renewables. Hence , oil need will be still the top position in future global energy product provision market.

On conclusion, in our energy market, commodities are the raw materials that form the foundation of the energy market. The three classes of commodities are agricultural, energy, metals. Through the price of energy commodities often influences the prices of the other two, such as crude oil, natural gas, coal and electricity. Hence, it explains that why we need to
know how to keep oil energy to avoid one day shortage problem occurs, because global any economic activities will be brought negative influence when oil energy can not be supplied to satisfy our any economic activities or daily lives useful needs. SO, it brings this question: What negative influences will be caused if one day oil had no enough supply to be provided
to any countries to use?

Oil shortage brings what social challenges

If one day, we are facing oil shortage to be supplied to any countries. Then, it will bring which aspects of social challenges to influence our daily lives, e.g. losing job or food shortage or any leisure can not be carried on, public transports lacking etc. different social challenges whether they will be influenced to occur be global oil shortage. If these any one challenge can be occur, how any why oil shortage will cause they occur and what the main factors can cause energy crisis occurrence. I shall attempt to explain as below:

First, we need to know what are the important factors that affect demand for oil, they may include transportation (both commercial and personal), population growth, and seasonal changes. For instance, oil use increases during busy summer travel seasons and in the winters, when more heating fuel is consumed as well as whether what factors may influence oil price. In fact, oil prices are influenced by three major factors: supply, demand and geopolitics. Second, we also need to know what energy crisis means . An energy crisis is any significant bottleneck in the supply of energy resources to an economy. In literature, it often refers to one of the energy sources used at a certain time and place, in particular, those that supply national electricity grids or those used as fuel in industrial development and population growth have led to a surge in the global demand for energy in recent years.

In fact, most energy crises have been caused by localized shortages, wars and market manipulation. Some have argued that government actions like tax hikes, nationalization of energy companies, and regulation of the energy sector, shift supply and demand of energy away from its economic equilibrium. However, the recent historical energy crisis listed below were not caused by such factors. Market failure is possible when monopoly manipulation of markets occurs. A crisis can develop due to industrial actions like union organized strikes and government embargoes. The cause may be over-consumption, aging infrastructure, choke point disruption or bottlenecks at oil refineries and port facilities that restrict fuel supply. An emergency may emerge during very cold winters due to increased consumption of energy. So, it seems that the main factor causes future possible energy crisis, it is not due to that oil can not be found from our earth oceans or lands natural environment factor . It is based on wars and market manipulation human immoral business behavioral factor. So, human needs to consider how to act correct behaviors to avoid energy crisis occurrence

.

However, if one day, energy shortage occurrence, whether what aspects of negative impacts will influence to our lives. I shall attempt to explain as below:

Why does oil may be shortage? Peak oil" is the period when the maximum rate of global petroleum extraction is reached, after which the rate of production enters terminal decline. It relates to a long-term decline in the available supply of petroleum. This, combined with increasing demand, significantly increases the worldwide prices of petroleum-derived products. Most significant is the availability and price of liquid fuel for transportation. So, oil shortage will bring these several aspects of negative and positive influences to our societies. They may include how to influence our societies as below:

On social economy and natural environment and tourism and transport aspect: Our air will have more fresh, ocean will be more clean and land can have more grass, flower and tree when our earth has no more oil resource can be extracted. Although it is on the good hand, but it also bring bad hand, such as the macroeconomic implications of a supply shock-induced energy crisis are large, because energy is the resource used to exploit all other resources. Oil price shocks can affect the rest of the economy through delayed business investment,] sectoral shifts in the labor market,[19] or monetary policy responses. When energy markets fail, an energy shortage develops. Electricity consumers may experience intentionally engineered rolling blackouts during periods of insufficient supply or unexpected power outages, regardless of the cause.

Industrialized nations are dependent on oil, and efforts to restrict the supply of oil would have an adverse effect on the economies of oil producers. For the consumer, the price of natural gas, gasoline (petrol) and diesel for cars and other vehicles rises. An early response from stakeholders is the call for reports, investigations and commissions into the price of fuels. There are also movements towards the development of more sustainable urban infrastructure.

In the market, new technology and energy efficiency measures become desirable for consumers seeking to decrease transport costs. January 30, 2008 Planet Ark. Examples include:

the growth of advanced biofuels.

innovations like the Dahon, a folding bicycle

modernized and electrifying passenger transport

Railway electrification systems and new engines such as the Ganz-Mavag locomotive

variable compression ratio for vehicles

Hence, we need to avoid to spend excess oil to cook at home, or drink cars on road, even avoid to listen music or watch television on day time etc. doing excess oil useful behaviors frequently. If we hope to avoid oil shortage will occur in futue one day.

CHAPTER TWO

What occurrence when we still excess waste oil use

I ensure that energy Crisis will be caused by eccess waste oil use ? What is Energy Crisis?

Energy crisis represents the huge demand for fuel which is increasing day by day. But the sources of energy are limited, and the stock limitation is more. For this reason, we all are facing a crisis, a crisis or a fear of having no fuel to produce electricity and use our favorite gadgets. Now the point is how many energy sources do we have? And how much fuel do these sources store for us? In a nutshell, energy can be of two kinds according to the sources. They are-

i) Non-renewable energy or Conventional energy.

ii) Renewable energy or Non-conventional energy.

What Are the Causes of Energy Crisis? They may include as below:

Overpopulation

Overconsumption of electricity

Misuse of electricity

Poor infrastructure

The low popularity of renewable energy

Wastage of fossil fuel

War

Terrorism

Nowadays we all are highly dependent on electronic equipment around us. From morning to night, we use hundreds of gadgets without even thinking about how much electrical energy these devices are consuming. For this reason, every country is trying to secure the future of its energy sector for its citizens. The population is increasing rapidly and as a result, the demand for power is increasing day by day. Another major reason behind the energy crisis is misuse of power. General people who are not very considerate about the importance of power make misuse of it every now and then.

What Are the Effects of Energy Crisis? They may include as below:

War at the middle east

Iraq crisis

Syria crisis

US sanctions on Iran

Setting up more and more nuclear reactors

However, the middle-east countries are facing so many issues only because of their mines. All the developed countries whether it is USA or Russia are trying heart and soul to control as many middle-east countries as possible. So that they can ensure uninterrupted fuel supply to their electricity generating plants.

Another problem occurring because of the energy crisis is that each developed country as well as the developing ones also are trying to establish nuclear power plants. Whereas we all know the dangers of nuclear reactors.

What Are the Solutions to Energy Crisis? They may include as below:

Popularize renewable energy sources

Population

control

Introduction of energy efficient gadgets

Proper energy management

Prevent misuse of energy

Energy simulation

Regular energy audit

Prevent climate change

Promote green economy

The first thing that we need is proper media coverage on the bad impacts of fossil fuel and make people aware of the causes of the energy crisis, its effect and what are the solutions of the energy crisis. Then general people will start to understand how vicious it would be for all of them. After that we can make renewable energy sources acceptable to them. Moreover, we should keep a close eye on the energy sector. Every year a huge amount of energy is lost only because of the lack of seriousness of the officials responsible for the supply of power. regular audit and manipulation should be arranged by the governments of every country.

Green economy should be encouraged by every state so that its financiers stop thinking about making revenue by tormenting the environment. Government should take proper steps to permit a proper budget to develop the renewable energy sector. Every country should establish an autonomous committee to research and decide which renewable energy source would be appropriate for them. And then according to the decision made by the committee renewable energy should be produced.

We all should learn about green technology to solve energy crisis.This planet is meant to be green and we all should let it be green. We all should promote tree plantation not deforestation. We have to keep in mind-

What do we plant when we plant a tree?
We plant a friend of sun and sky
We plant a flag of breezes free.

Global temperature increases on world scale have been a matter of concern and concern, on the other hand people are troubled by the rise in petroleum products. Within the country, the Prime Minister is presenting nuclear energy as

an inevitable alternative to meet the energy needs. As the cumulative reserves of coal and petroleum will decrease, the energy crisis will be deepened.

At present, about 70% of the electricity in India comes from coal based thermal power plants. Approximately 20% of the electricity is obtained from big hydro projects. But since the movement against big dams has started on the question of displacement, these projects have not been practicable since then. The life of a large dam is about 40 years. That is, the two biggest sources of power generation in India are coming to an end. Then where will our electricity come from?

At present, only 3% of the electricity is obtained from nuclear power in India. When the nuclear energy program was started here, its parent Homi Bhabha had predicted that by 1987, we would make 20-25,000 MW of electricity from this program. Obviously this program is not very successful. If the program of nuclear bombs was not connected with it then it would have been possible to close the program till now.

The nuclear energy program is also facing difficulties on the scale of the world. The main difficulty in this program is that scientists have no solution to safeguard the radioactive waste from the nuclear power plants. The waste from 104 nuclear power houses in the US is currently being kept in drums in the plant premises. The local public made such a huge opposition to the plan to bury the waste by making tunnels in the Ucca Hills of the state of Nevada that the US government has abandoned this idea at the moment.

This is the reason why there is no plan to set up a new nuclear power plant in the USA in 35 years. New nuclear power has ceased to be built in England, Canada and Germany over the last two-three decades. France, which today fulfills its 75% power requirement with nuclear energy, is only going to introduce a new factory in the coming days. In the coming two to three decades, France, which is presented as a successful example in the use of atomic energy, will fall in the percentage of contribution of nuclear energy in the generation of electricity. Japan is also looking for new sources of energy, especially transparent recovery resources.

A 2006 study by the Planning Commission of India stating that if India's nuclear deal is finally approved by crossing all obstacles and by 2020, we also make 40,000 megawatts of power, even then it will be able to generate electricity from India's total electricity Not to exceed 9% of the production Given the quality of the nuclear energy program so far, the actual production will probably be up to 5-7%. That is, we will have to rely on other sources for our 91-95% power. Thus, the Prime Minister says that nuclear energy is the only alternative in front of us to maintain India's 8-10% growth rate, it is unrealistic.

India has made remarkable progress in the field of wind energy over the last ten years. In the world, we have become the fourth largest country in terms of power generation from wind power. While the Department of Atomic Energy has been fully funded by the government for 60 years, in just ten years without the help of wind power, 5% electricity generation capacity in India has been established. That is, the power generation capacity of wind power has more than nuclear power. Wind power in India is likely to generate 45,000 MW power.

According to the Energy Engineering Administration, a US-based organization, about two-thirds of those plants will be found in electricity production in the world in the coming two to three decades. There can be two major sources of gas for India- Burma and Iran. Because the military ruler of Burma did not get angry, the Indian government did not openly support Aung San Sookie's democracy movement. But Burma has decided to sell its gas to China. In this way, Iran's gas which could come from the proposed Iran-Pakistan-India gas pipeline has become even more important to us. This is an agreement which is in the interest of the three countries, and between India and Pakistan, there is going to be such a thing after a long time, in which the interests of both of them are linked. This agreement will be more democratic and equitable than the Indo-US nuclear deal, and will be beneficial for the purpose of regional stability and peace.

For the next two to three decades, India will have to base its power generation on good quality coal and gas only. Even after coal, maybe carbon emissions from burning coal will be set to limit the use of coal. Carbon emissions in the use of gas is less than coal. For this, gas based technology will be more prevalent in the coming days.

But after three decades, we have to make the renewable resources the mainstay of our energy needs. In addition to wind, solar, biogas and micro hydro electricity will be the major ones. The way Japan and the European Union have decided that by 2050 they will create a low carbon emissions society, they should be ideal for us. America is not ready to impose any restrictions on this type of situation. Therefore, we will make a big mistake by considering America as an ideal. A responsible country should play its role in keeping ecological balance and keeping the environment clean.

The real energy challenge in front of India is how the majority of Indian nationals have access to electricity from villages and villages. In order to meet the needs of villages of India, they need cheap, micro / small, decentralized and local energy options. Renewable energy sources can also meet these needs better. We should also look at the fact that whenever it comes to meeting the energy requirements, we should not just think about the generation of electricity. Power without electricity can also be met. For example, the energy of solar energy can be cooked directly from the heat.Our objective should be that we develop alternatives to the needs of the society's energy in the wider public and environmental interest, with complete understanding and responsiveness from equitable misconceptions.

From Russia to Saudi Arabia, Iran to Venezuela, the list of crude oil supplies being curtailed or disrupted around the world is growing longer by the month. This story examines whether the market's biggest supply shifts are actually netting out into a global shortage of oil or not. The answer is a complex one, hinging on the type of crude in question and the time-frames selected.

The simplest supply measure is all the oil pulled out of the ground globally. On this view it does indeed look like global production has fallen sharply over the past six months, as the OPEC+ group of countries slashed supply, while the U.S. has toughened sanctions on the oil industries of Iran and Venezuela.

Figures published by the Energy Intelligence Group show that global oil production was 96.79 million barrels a day in April. That is a drop of more than 2 million barrels a day since the end of last year. But just a slightly a longer time-frame gives a different picture. If you compare April with a year earlier, production is actually up, by 570,000 barrels a day — pretty much in line with oil demand growth. While such a broad look at global oil production data offers some insight, it misses a lot of important detail.

Most of the new refineries built in Asia and the Middle East in recent years were designed to run on a diet of heavy, sour crudes. These barrels feature a high proportion of large hydrocarbon molecules that need to be broken down into smaller ones to make high-value transport fuels. They also tend to contain relatively high concentrations of sulfur that have to be removed to meet anti-pollution regulations.

Where is the growth in oil supply location has been? Booming production from the U.S. Permian Basin has driven a surge in the supply of light crude, which was up year-on-year by more than 1.8 million barrels a day in April. By contrast, the increase since the end of 2018 has been much smaller, at 160,000 barrels a day.

The picture for heavy crude is completely different. Slumping output from Venezuela, where years of mismanagement and under-investment have been compounded by the impact of U.S. sanctions on the state oil company, has driven a sharp drop in global supply, both year-on-year and year-to-date. The impact of Venezuela's difficulties has been exacerbated by continuing declines in Mexico's oil production, which was previously expected to be reversed this year.

Saudi oil production, which surged in the second half of 2018, is now back where it was a year ago. Initially, it more than offset the decline in Iranian supply that resulted from the snap-back of U.S. oil sanctions. But since January, a drop in Iran's output hasn't been covered by increases in medium crude production elsewhere.

Sanctions waivers, issued to eight buyers of Iranian crude, were not renewed by the U.S. when they expired in early May and that will keep Iran's output under further pressure in the coming months. For now, Saudi Arabia appears unwilling to boost its own supply, preferring instead to push for an extension of the OPEC+ output restraint.

So is there an oil shortage? There's certainly no shortage of light crude, but the picture is very different for the medium and heavies. The 2 million barrel a day drop in total production since the end of 2018 has all been medium and heavy, with little additional light oil to offset the decline in that period. But over the longer time-frame, rising light crude output has more than offset the declines elsewhere, giving a small net increase.

When human excess to waste oil use , waste oil regeneration process and pollution occurrence will be caused as below:

View Larger Image , among the several methods of waste oil treatment, there are two types that are more commonly used now. One is the production of clean liquid fuels or road oils that remove heavy metals, and the other is the production of regenerative lubricants. Both types of treatment methods can meet environmental and economic requirements.

The recycling process itself also needs to pay attention to environmental pollution problems. Some regeneration unit processes are essentially free of environmental pollution, such as distillation and hydrogenation. Some regenerative unit processes will bring more or less environmental pollution, such as flocculated waste liquid, alkali washing and alkali washing waste water, and adsorbed and refined waste adsorbent. If discharged or discarded without treatment, it will also be environmentally friendly. Cause certain pollution. Some regenerative unit processes, such as sulfuric acid refining, have a greater impact on the environment, and the resulting acid slag, if discarded casually, will cause serious pollution to the environment, and the resulting sulfur dioxide gas is also harmful to living things.

In recent years, it has been starting from environmental protection and attaching importance to the waste lubricating oil recycling industry. Of course, it is not tolerable that waste oil regeneration will cause new pollution to the environment. Therefore, in recent years, some sulfuric acid refining devices have been discontinued, and a pollution-free regeneration process has been developed. Even if the refinery that still retains the sulfuric acid refinery is found, it has found a way to properly treat the acid residue so that it does not harm the environment.

Hence, the development of a new pollution-free recycling process to replace sulfuric acid refining, the most successful is to take the thin film evaporation under high vacuum and low temperature, steam the base oil fraction without any cracking, and then through the clay or hydrogenation refining, become Good quality recycled base oil. Some large-scale waste oil refineries now use pollution-free processes. However, many large factories and many small and medium-sized factories are still using the sulfuric acid-white clay process and adopting an effective three-waste treatment method to make environmental protection acceptable. As for re-purification, since there is not much pollution problem, it can meet environmental protection requirements with a little attention. So, human excess oil useful behavior , it can cause natural pollution to our natural environment easily. We need to consider pollution issue is due to our excess oil useful behavior.

CHAPTER THREE

Energy consumer useful behavior or oil shortage influences oil supply changes

How Do Supply and Demand Affect the Oil Industry?

The law of supply and demand primarily affects the oil industry by determining the price of the "black gold." Expectations about the price of oil are the major determining factors in how companies in the industry allocate their resources. Prices create incentives that influence behavior. This behavior eventually feeds back into supply and demand to determine the price of oil.

The most striking feature of the oil market is the low price elasticity of demand. In fact, the supply of oil is also fairly inelastic. Oil price swings tend to be dramatic and often impact the rest of the economy.

The Low Elasticity of Demand to oil market

The most striking feature of the oil market is the low price elasticity of demand. That means demand for oil is not very responsive to changes in prices. It is easy to see this by looking at your own life. If you have a car, you usually continue driving to work, going to stores, and visiting friends regardless of the price of gasoline. Your demand for oil does not change very much based on the price, and it works the same way for others. Even people who use less oil have a relatively inelastic demand for it. Someone who uses mass transit or lives close to work will not move out to the suburbs and buy a gas-guzzling SUV just because the oil price fell. At most, lower oil prices will induce people to take more vacations in the short run. Oil prices have a strong impact on airline fares and the cost of driving across the country.

In the long run, businesses and consumers can adapt to changing oil prices. Companies might react somewhat more quickly to improve the energy efficiency of their operations. Consumers have to be at the right point in their lives to make changes. When someone is ready to buy a new car, fuel efficiency becomes more important when oil prices are high. The low price elasticity of demand for oil is quite different from the demand for other goods and services, even other types of energy. For example, higher natural gas prices can lead to more use of solar, coal, and oil for generating electricity. However, most automobiles in 2020 still required gasoline, and therefore oil, to function.

The Low Elasticity of Supply to oil market

As a general rule, supply is less responsive to price changes than demand. However, the supply of oil is fairly inelastic, even by the standards of supply curves.

First, it helps to consider why supply is generally less elastic than demand, particularly in the short run. There is a fixed supply of goods at any given moment, and demand must adapt. For instance, the sudden increase in people working from home during the coronavirus crisis created a shortage of consumer paper products at stores in 2020. People previously got toilet paper, facial tissues, and paper towels from different companies via their employers while at work. In the short term, consumers simply had to reduce their demand.

The supply of oil is even less elastic than most other goods because of the specialized investments that are often needed to extract oil. Much of the equipment that is used to mine gold or silver can be diverted to mining platinum or palladium as prices shift. However, expensive equipment used for hydraulic fracturing and offshore drilling often cannot be used for anything else. As a result, oil companies may take years to develop oil fields when prices are high. Furthermore, they often have to continue producing oil even when prices fall because the equipment has no other uses.

Boom and Bust to oil industry

Since both supply and demand for oil are not very responsive to price changes, oil price swings tend to be dramatic. Furthermore, oil price changes often impact the rest of the economy. Sudden disruptions in the oil supply can cause recessions, while a decline in the oil price can fuel an economic boom.

Most people in developed countries need oil to go to work, school, or even to the store to get food. We don't want to give up on any of that and are willing to pay more, but everyone else is in the same boat. As a result, oil prices have to go up a lot to get consumers to change their behavior. Oil firms also need to take in those big profits to fund the development of more oil fields, which is very costly and high risk.

High oil prices mean a boom for the oil industry and often a bust for other industries. Everyone who uses a traditional automobile suddenly has to pay more for gas, so they have less disposable income available for other goods. The impact of higher gas prices is often higher for people who have lower incomes.

On the other hand, low oil prices usually mean a bust for oil firms and a boom for other industries. The oil companies find their costly investments in fracking and offshore oil wells becoming unprofitable. Other businesses suddenly see their energy expenses fall and their profits rise. Lower transportation costs tend to benefit trade and boost commerce. Finally, consumers see their disposable incomes rise as fuel costs fall.

Real-Life energy users general behavior

An example of the impact of high oil prices occurred around 2011. At that time, the cost of crude soared above $100. Massive investments poured into the sector via credit and new companies. Production increased in response to high prices, especially with innovations in hydraulic fracturing and oil sands. These investments could only be justified based on high oil prices and eventually contributed to an oil glut in 2014. But the high cost of oil also led to great improvements in efficiency, which decreased demand for energy on a per-person basis. There was also deflationary pressure due to tighter monetary policy in the United States. Given the supply and demand dynamics, oil prices plummeted in 2014. It is one good example to explain high oil cost can improve oil manufacturing efficiencym when oil supply can be increase, so it cause that productin increased in repsonse to oil high price occurrence.

How does oil supply affect world demand?

The ability to supply oil for world demand affects the ultimate price of the product. The world's supply of oil centers around the capacity of reserves. Reflected as the available supply, oil reserves are most often expressed in terms of "proven reserves."

How does economic growth affect crude oil?

Economic growth is one of the biggest factors affecting petroleum product—and therefore crude oil—demand. Growing economies increase demand for energy in general and especially for transporting goods and materials from producers to consumers. Why is the oil price fluctuating? For example, in May 2011, the flooding of the Mississippi River also led to oil price fluctuation. From a global perspective, political instability in the Middle East causes oil prices to fluctuate, as the region accounts for the lion's share of the worldwide oil supply.

What factors Cause Oil Prices to Fluctuate?

It may include these impacts, such as: Supply and Demand Impact, Natural Disasters, Politics Weigh, Production Costs, Storage Impact and Interest Rate Impact.

Oil is a commodity, and as such, it tends to see larger fluctuations in price than more stable investments, such as stocks and bonds. There are several influences on oil prices. Oil prices are influenced by a variety of factors, particularly the decisions about output made by producers like OPEC, the Organization of Petroleum Exporting Countries, independent petro-states like Russia and private oil-producing firms like Exxon-Mobile.

Natural disaster can influence oil price changes

Like any product, the laws of supply and demand influence prices; a combination of stable demand and oversupply has put pressure on oil prices over the last five years. Natural disasters that could potentially disrupt production, and political unrest in oil-producing countries all impact pricing. For example, the COVID-19 crisis is like a natural disaster because it adversely affected demand as people world-wide drove and flew less. Production costs influence prices, along with storage capacity; although less impactful, the direction of interest rates can also influence the price of commodities.

Why does OPEC Influences Prices ?

OPEC, or the Organization of Petroleum Exporting Countries, is the main influencer of fluctuations in oil prices. OPEC is a consortium that, as of 2020, is made up of 13 countries: Algeria, Angola, Congo, Equatorial Guinea, Gabon, Iran, Iraq, Kuwait, Libya, Nigeria, Saudi Arabia, the United Arab Emirates, and Venezuela.1

According to 2018 statistics, OPEC controls almost 80% of the world's supply of oil reserves.2 The consortium sets production levels to meet global demand and can influence the price of oil and gas by increasing or decreasing production. Before 2014, OPEC vowed to keep the price of oil above $100 a barrel for the foreseeable future, but midway through that year, the price of oil began to tumble. It fell from a peak of above $100 a barrel to below $50 a barrel.3 OPEC was the major cause of cheap oil in that instance, as it refused to cut oil production, leading to the tumble in prices.

In the Spring of 2020, oil prices collapsed to historic and unprecedented lows. Futures contracts for West Texas Intermediate crude were negative on April 20, 2020—there were no buyers for those oil contracts. Several reasons were given for this price anomaly. First, lockdowns to fight the COVID-19 pandemic around the world decimated oil demand. Simultaneously, a dispute between OPEC member Saudi Arabia and Russia (not an OPEC member) led to a flood of supply hitting the market. President Trump tried to broker a deal to cut production, but it was not implemented in time to prop up oil prices.

How Supply and Demand factor Impact to oil market

As with any commodity, stock, or bond, the laws of supply and demand cause oil prices to change. When supply exceeds demand, prices fall; the inverse is also true, when demand outpaces supply. The dramatic drop in oil prices in 2014 fall has been attributed to lower demand for oil in Europe and China, coupled with a steady supply of oil from OPEC.4 The excess supply of oil caused oil prices to fall sharply. While supply and demand impact oil prices, it is actually oil futures that set the price of oil. A futures contract for oil is a binding agreement that gives a buyer the right to buy a barrel of oil at a set price in the future. As spelled out in the contract, the buyer and seller of the oil are required to complete the transaction on a specific date.

The COVID-19 Natural Disasters Demand Shock of 2020 factor impacts oil share market

Oil futures markets were hit with a historical anomaly on April 20, 2020, when the May WTI Crude futures contract fell to negative $40.32. One way of understanding how the futures contract could be negative is to understand that the cost of storing oil was, at that time, very high due to months of oversupply and the total lack of demand brought on by the COVID-19 pandemic. Futures traders were willing to pay to offload their futures contracts so they would not have to take physical delivery of the oil. (There isn't a lot of oil storage space in financial trading companies.)

The situation where near-term prices are lower than futures farther out is called contango, and news outlets called oil's contango on April 20th a "supercontango." Usually, contango refers to a situation where arbitrageurs buy a commodity at its spot price and roll it into a futures contract at a higher price. But because so many traders were desperate to dump their May contracts—a situation probably made worse by oil ETFs that automatically roll forward contracts—the market mechanism was overwhelmed.

Natural disasters are another factor that can cause oil prices to fluctuate. For example, when Hurricane Katrina struck the southern U.S. in 2005, affecting almost 20% of the U.S. oil supply, it caused the price per barrel of oil to rise by $13.5 6 In May 2011, the flooding of the Mississippi River also led to oil price fluctuation. From a global perspective, political instability in the Middle East causes oil prices to fluctuate, as the region accounts for the lion's share of the worldwide oil supply. For example, in July 2008, the price of a barrel of oil reached $128 due to the unrest and consumer fear about the wars in both Afghanistan and Iraq.

The COVID-19 pandemic is another example of a natural disaster, but unlike nearly all other natural disasters that raise the price of oil by creating a supply shock, the COVID-19 disaster created a demand shock. Many flights—both international and domestic—were canceled on orders of governments to close borders. As a result, gasoline consumption in the U.S. fell off a cliff. Consequently, gasoline refiners didn't want to take oil that they couldn't process for sale, and oil reserves began to pile up at the WTI storage facility in Cushing, Oklahoma (where oil is stored for delivery in the U.S). In response to the crisis, major oil producers sidelined production. It is expected that many small producers will go bankrupt.

The United States consumes almost one-fourth of the world's oil.

Production Costs, Storage Have Impact to oil market

Production costs can cause oil prices to rise or fall as well. While oil in the Middle East is relatively cheap to extract, oil in Canada in Alberta's oil sands is more costly.9 Once the supply of cheap oil is exhausted, the price could conceivably rise, if the only remaining oil is in the tar sands.

U.S. production also directly affects the price of oil. With so much oversupply in the industry, a decline in production decreases overall supply and increases prices. As of 2019, the U.S. has an average daily production level of 12 million barrels of oil.10 That average production, while volatile, can trend downward. Consistent weekly drops put upward pressure on oil prices as a result. Oil diverted into storage has grown exponentially, and key hubs have seen their storage tanks filling up rather quickly. As of mid-April 2020, the storage hub at Cushing holds roughly 60 million barrels—with a total capacity of 76 million barrels.

More importantly, given the demand crisis created by the COVID-19 pandemic, the rate at which oil has filled up reserves prompted oil majors and oil-producing governments to slash production. In this unprecedented environment, the only winners are companies who store oil, including shipping companies with tankers who have been able to raise prices for oil storage. OPEC is widely seen as the most influential player in oil price fluctuations, but basic supply and demand factors, production costs, political turmoil, and even interest rates can play a significant role in the price of oil.

Interest Rate Impact to oil market

While views are mixed, the reality is that oil prices and interest rates have some correlation between their movements. However, they are not tightly correlated. In truth, many factors affect the direction of both interest rates and oil prices. Sometimes those factors are related, sometimes they affect each other, and sometimes there's no rhyme or reason to what happens.

One of the basic theories stipulates that increasing interest rates raise consumers' and manufacturers' costs, which reduces the amount of time and money people spend driving. Fewer people on the road translates to less demand for oil, which can cause oil prices to drop. In this instance, we'd call this an inverse correlation.

By this same theory, when interest rates drop, consumers and companies are able to borrow and spend money more freely, which drives up demand for oil. The greater the usage of oil, the more consumers bid up the price.

Another economic theory proposes that rising or high-interest rates help strengthen the dollar against other countries' currencies. When the dollar is strong, American oil companies can buy more oil with every U.S. dollar spent, ultimately passing the savings on to consumers. Likewise, when the value of the dollar is low against foreign currencies, the relative strength of U.S. dollars means buying less oil than before. This, of course, can contribute to oil becoming costlier to the U.S., which consumes almost 20% of the world's oil.

All of these oil demand and supply can influence oil price changes.

Factors Affecting Demand & Supply of Oil Prices may include these factors as below:

Crude oil supplies are crucial to the operation of developed countries, with 84,249,000 barrels consumed globally each day as of 2009. Because of the importance of oil supplies, fluctuation of oil prices can have a great effect on the global economy. The standard economic principle of supply and demand, based around the concept that the price of a product is directly related to relationship of supply related to consumer demand, applies to global oil prices and the resulting effects on worldwide economics.

Increased Oil Consumption factor

As the world's population grows, global oil demand increases accordingly. According to the U.S. Energy Information Administration's 2009 statistics, the U.S. led the world in global oil consumption with more than 18 million 42-gallon barrels consumed each day across the country. Oil demand is highest in developed countries, with China, Japan and India trailing the U.S. in oil consumption.

Oil Reserves factor

The ability to supply oil for world demand affects the ultimate price of the product. The world's supply of oil centers around the capacity of reserves. Reflected as the available supply, oil reserves are most often expressed in terms of "proven reserves." Proven reserves are expected quantities of oil, determined through analysis performed by geologists and engineers, that can be extracted with a high level of success using current methods. The potential of proven reserves can be increased through technological advances and further exploration of supply locations, as well as economic conditions that favor oil production.

Exchange Rates factor

World exchange rates directly affect the worldwide price of oil in terms of how the cost is reflected in national markets. The declining value of the U.S. dollar increases the impact oil prices have on the American economy. When oil prices increase, Americans must pay even more U.S. dollars to buy oil due to the reduced value of the currency. In cases of appreciation, such as when the euro strengthened in value, increased oil prices can be canceled out by a more valuable form of money.

Environmental Factors

The environment can have a strong effect on the global price of oil, in terms of drastically changing the ability to produce oil supplies. For example, in 2004, a number of devastating hurricanes hit off the southeast coast of the U.S. These hurricanes damaged oil supply facilities and reduced the flow of crude oil supplies to the U.S. Applying the economic principle of supply and demand, the decrease in oil production could not meet with consumer needs and caused an increase in oil prices.

Political Factors

Whenever a major oil producing country is affected by political conflict, that nation's ability to continue production will be affected. For example, the 2002 political strikes in Venezuela had a detrimental effect on the major oil producer's supplies, causing worldwide shortages and ultimately increasing prices due to disparities with demand. The Iraq war provided another incident of oil price increases, as the nation's production capability was affected due to military conflicts and terrorist attacks.

Speculation Factor

Outside of physical supply of oil reserves, the financial market has the ability to change oil prices through speculation. Essentially, this means financial traders speculate on oil supplies through contracts that are for future shipments, rather than those currently being distributed. This speculation can lead to traders working to raise or lower the price of oil to receive desired profits on purchased contracts.

Consequently, all these external environment factors can influence global oil supply and demand how to change in global oil energy market.

CHAPTER FOUR

Oil shortage how influences energy user behavior changes

Oil shortage may bring changes in transport behaviour changes during the Covid-19 crisis when we feel afraid oil shortage problem will be caused by Covid-19 disease global occurrence. How Covid -19 disease influences we feel afraid that oil shortage will be caused as well as how it can influence global human oil useful behavior begins to change , I shall explain as below :

The restrictions put in place to limit the diffusion and impacts of Covid-19 have had a widespread impact on people's lives, and the way energy is used across entire economies. One of the biggest impacts has been the reduction in passenger transport demand, due to a combination of government lockdowns and fears of contracting and spreading the virus when using mass transport modes. While freight transport has also been reduced, the drivers of freight activity during the current crisis are complex, driven by both supply- and demand-side factors, and in the latter, by the need to keep essential services operating. In contrast, passenger transport, (for both leisure and business travel) is often optional, and more influenced by people's decision-making processes. Hence, Covid 19 disease can impact oil need to public transport need reduces because many people do not need to catch any public transport, e.g. bus, taxi, train, tram, underground train, ferry to go to office to work because their employers do not want many staffs work in small office working environment in order to avoid COVID 19 disease impacts to their businesses. However, they can work at home by internet. Hence, it implies that any countries public transport services do not need much oil or gas energy for their transport tools. Then, oil price may be influenced to reduce , due to oil/gas demand reduces to any countries public transport services in this COVID 19 disease occurrence time.

The crisis has affected all forms of transport, from cars, and public transport in cities, to buses, trains and planes nationally and internationally. Global road transport activity was almost 50% below the 2019 average by the end of March 2020 and commercial flight activity almost 75% below 2019 by mid-April 2020. Public transport has also been affected. For example, the strict lockdown imposed in the UK in March 2020 has led to a 95% decrease in underground journeys in London. This is supported by data1 from one popular transport planning smartphone app showing that trips are down by over 90% since the crisis began in many of the world's major cities.

How and why Covid-19 is changing our behaviour and transport energy use patterns.

For the energy sector, this trend has had huge knock-on effects for oil consumption, contributing to a 5% decrease in demand in the first quarter of 2020. With passenger transport responsible for around 40% of final oil demand and 15% of global energy-related carbon emissions, any crisis-induced changes to way we travel will have significant global implications, if changes to transport behaviours become permanent after lockdowns are lifted. Therefore, a key question for the energy sector is whether changes to transport behaviours during the crisis may result in a permanent change in behaviour (and transport energy use) or if transport patterns will revert to 'business as usual' when the crisis ends. Research has shown that disruptions can be a catalyst for shifts towards more sustainable transport behaviours but avoiding a return to pre-crisis behaviours requires governments to take decisive actions. While the current crisis is unprecedented, in terms of the scale of impacts and government responses, examining past crises can be instructive in informing policy makers how people's behaviours can change during and immediately following a crisis, and what sort of policy options are available to government to incentivise certain behaviours and discourage others.

In recent decades, there have been a number of crises—including multiple health and terrorism-related crises—that have caused sudden changes in transport demand, as people make significant changes to transport patterns, either in response to changes necessitated by transport disruptions, or perceived risks of travelling. This is particularly true for non-essential travel and in relatively wealthy countries where people have access to remote working facilities or alternative, private forms of transport. For other people, the decision to cease commuting during a crisis may not be an option at all.

In fact, mass transport, which brings people into close proximity with each other, is where some the most tangible behavioural changes manifest during a crisis, particularly air transport, which is generally perceived as being non-essential. For example, the Severe Acute Respiratory Syndrome (SARS) crisis of 2003 reduced demand for passenger air transport in the affected regions by about 35% at the height of the crisis. Demand continued to be below business-as-usual levels six months after the epidemic had eased, resulting in an 8% annual decrease of revenue passenger kilometres. The SARS crisis also affected non-essential trips on public transport. In Taipei, there were half as many underground trips during the peak of the SARS epidemic and it took four months for passenger numbers to return pre-crisis levels.

Several other viruses emerged since the SARS outbreak that affected aviation demand including the Avian Flu outbreaks of 2005 and 2013 and Middle Eastern Respiratory Syndrome in 2015. In these cases, demand for air travel bounced back relatively quickly. However, it is reasonable to assume that the public's response to Covid-19 will more closely resemble the response to SARS, as the scale of the impacts and the perceived risks of contagion are much greater compared to more recent pandemics. Already, surveys of public attitudes to risk suggest that people in most countries will take time before feeling confident enough to travel again. In another survey, two out of five passengers in major aviation markets want to wait for at least six months before travelling again.

How air travel market influences oil demand and price changes when COVID 19 disease occurs? How terrorist attacks occur to underground train stations to influence electricity price and electricity demand change?

On how air travel influences oil demand and price aspect, from a behavioural perspective, the speed at which air travel demand resumes may also depend on whether responses to the virus permanently change the way we travel. For example, increased health checks may help to provide a sense of security for some passengers. Alternatively, if such procedures make flying a more complicated and time-consuming mode of transport, potential air travellers could be dissuaded from flying. The combined impact of passengers' perceptions of danger and inconvenience on transport demand was demonstrated in 2001, following the September 11 terrorist attacks (9/11). After 9/11 there was a large drop in demand for air transport, as business and leisure passengers reassessed both the risks and inconvenience of flying after new security precautions were introduced. Studies showed that the overall impact on air transport was long-lasting: despite bouncing back, some analysts estimate that US domestic air passenger travel was over -7% lower in the five years after the attacks than it would have been, had they not occurred.

In China, the domestic aviation market is starting to rebound as domestic travel restrictions are eased. However, the extent to which the Covid-19 crisis will affect global aviation demand in the longer term remains to be seen. Modelling by the International Civil Aviation Organisation (ICAO) suggests the short-term (within 12 months) impact will be a severe drop in passengers under most scenarios.If and when demand for passenger air transport returns to pre-crisis levels will depend on a range of factors including perception of risk, cost, convenience, and the availability of alternative transport modes, all of which affect people's mobility decisions. Government policies (discussed below) can influence each of these factors. Concerning business travel, Covid-19 could be different from previous crises, if companies determine that replacing business trips with videoconferencing is more feasible as technologies mature. Thus, crises can result in long-lasting reductions in transport demand, especially where transport is not considered essential. In addition to direct demand reductions for particular modes of transport, previous crises also show that people often adopt new transport practices during and immediately following a crisis, which can sometimes become permanent, depending on a range of factors. A clear example of modal shifts in response to a crisis came after the London terrorist attacks in July 2005, when a series of bombs exploded in three London underground trains and one bus, killing 56 people and injuring another 700. Although the damaged underground lines reopened within weeks, the attacks had longer lasting impacts on the city's commuting patterns. Londoners avoided underground journeys for months and partly switched to other modes of transport such as cycling. Bike retailers in London reported that sales quadrupled in the week following the attack and bike use increased by 13% from June to July. Cycling trips remained high until the end of 2005, with a 9% annual increase in registered trips compared to the previous year, whereas car, bus and underground use decreased. Hence, trerrorist attacks to any countries underground train public transport service, it will impact many passengers choose other public transport tools to catch. Then, the electricty energy will reduce demand to global public underground train public transport service , if terrorist attacks occur to many countries' underground train stations. Consequently, global electricity price may be influenced to reduce, due to demand to global underground trains service providers do not need to use much electricity to provide underground trains to catch big number of passengers if terrorist attacts occurs to global many underground train stations frequently.

How individual active transport habit influences oil price and oil demand to transport aspect ?

How cyclists active transport behavior influences oil energy supplying to transport demand and oil price changes?

Previous crises have spurred long-term shifts in transport preferences when supported by other factors. For many commuters, the bombings may have acted as a catalyst for switching to active transport modes, convinced after experiencing benefits such as cost and time savings over public transport or better health. However, other factors also contributed. For example, the introduction of the congestion charge for private vehicles entering central London had contributed to a strong increase in bike use since 2003 and more than half of the respondents in a 2004 survey mentioned the charge as a key trigger for cycling more.

The availability of infrastructure was also key to keeping attracting new cyclists in the years following the bombings. For example, a growing network of dedicated 'quietways' and fully-protected 'cycle superhighways' (since 2010) has been crucial in attracting additional first-time cyclists by providing safer conditions.

It should also be noted that despite the increase in cyclists stimulated by the crisis, the overall impact on commuting patterns was relatively insignificant in terms of long-term changes to transport energy demand: bicycles still only accounted for 2.5% of all trips in London in 2018 despite the 2.6-fold increase in bike rides since 2000.

Nonetheless, the scale of the Covid-19 crisis could stimulate even larger and longer lasting effects on mobility patterns compared with crises like the London Bombings, depending on how the public perceives risk. That is, if the perceived risk of contracting Covid-19 on mass transport modes seemingly outweighs the safety risks associated with other modes, people might choose to switch transport behaviours for a longer period, a phenomenon known as 'dread behaviour'.

Already reports are emerging of shifts to active transport modes out of necessity, as social distancing measures reduce public transport use. Cities such as New York and Philadelphia were reporting a substantial increase in cycling (the number of cyclists more than doubling in the latter) during the beginning of the pandemic, made more attractive by unusually empty streets and better air quality. The UK's Association of Cycle Traders reported a boom in mending as people retrieve old bicycles from their sheds, while one of the largest bike suppliers in the United States ran out of stock on some of its top selling models as sales have surged. After the lockdowns are lifted, these shifts could become more permanent if commuters' risk calculus suggests such modes pose less risk than the alternatives. In Wuhan, where the Covid-19 outbreak first emerged, since the lockdown was lifted, bike-sharing services have witnessed up to tenfold increases in ride orders compared to pre-crisis levels. Of course, as the perceived risks of travelling via public transport linger, people are also likely to seek out more energy intensive transport options than cycling, often for purely practical reasons. In many cities, private cars were a more dominant form of transport prior to the Covid-19 crisis and previous crises suggest car usage could spike following this crisis. For example, after 9/11, private vehicle use increased, as people sought to reduce their exposure to potential terrorist targets on mass transport. Ironically, such dread behaviour may have led to higher exposure to death by car accident.

Even in London, dread behaviour after the 2005 bombings stimulated some degree of switching from public transport to fossil-fuel powered private vehicles, in the form of motorcycles. Research suggests one of the secondary impacts of the bombings was a 7-11% increase in vehicle particulate emissions, with long-term negative impacts on Londoners' health.

As countries begin to lift their lockdowns, it will be important to remember how people responded in previous crises and already signs are emerging that some degree of switching to more energy-intensive transport modes is likely. In one survey of consumer sentiment, 20% of people who regularly used buses, subways or trains said they no longer would, while 17% of people indicated they would use their car more due to Covid-19. Fears of Covid-19 have helped increase car sales above 2019 levels in Korea in both March and April 2020, while in Beijing, morning peak-hour traffic has recently been above normal levels as commuters opted to drive over risking public transport.

These early manifestations of dread behaviour suggest that far from ushering in the beginning of peak oil demand, behaviours in response to Covid-19 could spark a rebound in transport-related oil use when countries end their lockdowns. Governments will need to help people avoid unintended consequences that can flow from dread behaviour and more accurately assess the risks associated with their transport choices, including virus exposure, transport accidents, and the economic, environmental and health impacts of congestion.

The examples discussed above show that crises can stimulate lasting changes in mobility patterns, with both positive and negative impacts. As new mobility patterns emerge with this crisis—such as even more widespread increases in bicycle use than previous crises—building on the lessons learned in the past could help ensure sustainable transport behaviours persist. Most importantly, previous crises show that supporting policies are needed to promote sustainable behaviours and avoid negative consequences that can flow from people's calculus of risk in the wake of a crisis. At a time when people will be feeling vulnerable, policies that increase trust in the safety of sustainable transport options are particularly important.

Hence, some countries people began to like to ride bicycles to go to offices, schools or anywhere, it is possible on health reason, sport reason, reducing transport expenditure reason. Hence, it will bring indirect influences to transport oil demand reduces and oil price reduces.

Investments into good quality public transport infrastructure and new and improved cycling networks can make sustainable modes of transport more attractive and safer, especially in the wake of a crisis. Support for public transport agencies to maintain infrastructure and service provision after the lockdown will be particularly crucial in this crisis, as several are experiencing significant revenue losses due to reduced ridership during the lockdown period.

For cycling, the provision of infrastructure such well delineated cycleways and quality end-of-trip facilities has been proven to be one of the best ways to increase cycling uptake by bolstering safety and convenience. Infrastructure to boost safety is especially important for increasing cycling uptake in under-represented segments of the population such as women, who perceive traffic safety differently. Evidence from the London bombings demonstrates the need to provide infrastructure to keep cyclists safe as lockdowns are lifted and traffic volumes increase: the rise in bicycle commutes after the 2005 attacks reportedly led to an increase in cyclist casualties. London has since completed several major cycling infrastructure projects that have helped to increase cycling safety and participation, including dedicated cycling 'super highways' and cycle hire schemes which are helping to create a 'critical mass' of cyclists.

Already more than 150 cities have provided dedicated cycling and walking infrastructure in anticipation of the post-crisis surge in traffic as of late April 2020. Bogotá is opening 80 km of roads to cyclists, building on experience from car-free Sundays on most of these streets, while Lima is constructing 300 km of bike lanes within 100 days. In Paris, 650 km of cycleways are to be built, connecting the city centre with the suburbs—including temporary 'corona bike lanes'. Oakland has converted 10% of its streets into 'slow streets' closed to through motor traffic, while other cities are widening sidewalks to accommodate more pedestrians in a safe way. Where feasible, converting such temporary infrastructure into more permanent structures would help to ensure positive behaviours induced by the crisis continue into the future.

Ensuring public trust in the safety of public transport will be difficult, as people will likely continue to avoid close physical contact with others. However, maintaining the quality and safety of public transport services in the post lockdown period will be crucial to ensure people do not lose faith in public transport systems in the longer term. Governments will need to ensure public transport systems have the resources to maintain reliability standards while also catering to commuters perceptions of safety, through measures to maintain a level of social distancing. This may involve increasing the frequency of services and publishing real-time updates on public transport congestion to allow for commuters to travel in relatively less crowded vehicles, for example. Other evolving practices around the world include the compulsory use of protective facemasks, sanitiser provision and more frequent cleaning of trains and buses, temperature checks at metro entrances and automatic opening of all doors at any station to prevent direct contact.

Price and regulatory policies factor incentivises less energy need to transport and influences oil price reduces and oil demand reduces

Pricing and regulatory policies can help incentivise less energy-intensive transport behaviours when the crisis ends .

When the current crisis ends, a major determinant of whether people stick with public and active transport modes over more energy-intensive transport modes will be the relative cost of different transport options. While oil prices have now dropped to an historical low, creating a stronger incentive to drive and fly, policies can help to ensure the right balance of costs and benefits as demand rebounds. Similarly, pricing on-street parking can generate revenues for reinvestment in sustainable transport while disincentivising private vehicle use and reducing congestion. For example, drivers searching for parking are responsible for a third of the vehicle traffic in urban centres during peak hours—especially in areas with unpaid, or under-priced, parking.

Positive incentives for active transport modes can also drive greater uptake. In several European countries, cyclists can claim rebates for every kilometre cycled into work. For instance, in the Netherlands, where cycling rates are the highest in the world, cyclists can claim €0.19 for every kilometre cycled to work. In response to the Covid-19 crisis, the French government announced a Sustainable Mobility Package, which includes up to €400 per year, tax free, for employees who can prove the use of sustainable transport modes, including car-sharing and cycling.

In the aviation sector, the absence of a price on the negative environmental externalities of air travel is one reason for the continuing low cost of air tickets, helping to drive strong demand for flights over more environmentally sustainable transport modes. Especially in markets where domestic jet fuels are not subject to carbon pricing, accelerated phase-outs of fossil fuel subsidies—such as exemptions from taxes on kerosene fuel—could help to level the playing field for less energy-intensive forms of transport. In the wake of the Covid-19 crisis, some governments are now pursuing interventions that would remove cheap but energy-intensive options from travellers' decision-making entirely. For example, the French government recently announced that bailouts for Air France would be contingent on the airline ceasing to provide domestic flights for trips that could be completed by train in under 2 hours and 30 minutes.

Regulatory instruments can also be crucial to supporting more sustainable transport behaviours. For example, vehicle speed limits and overtaking laws can significantly affect cycling safety, and importantly, perceptions of safety, by reducing 'near misses'. In response to the Covid-19 stimulated increases in cycling, some cities are already responding with regulations designed to increase cyclist safety. Brussels, for instance, has reduced speed limits to 20 km/h in the city centre. Traffic rules prioritising cyclists and pedestrians in shared road spaces are another option, especially at crowded junctions.

Household environment protectional behavior influences oil demand reduces and oil price reduces

Another lesson from energy conservation campaigns in the household sector is that campaigns promoting actions that are relatively easy to take are more likely to be successful. This was demonstrated during the Fukushima nuclear crisis, when Japanese households managed to achieved large and sustained cuts in electricity use in response to the government's Setsuden campaign. Analysis has since found that the actions most likely to be taken up were those that did not require either frequent efforts or considerable discomfort. Stimulus spending can be used to support less energy intensive transport modes

Finally, while governments are in the process of designing and rolling out stimulus programmes to reduce the economic impacts of the crisis, there is an opportunity to direct stimulus spending to the measures already discussed, particularly transport infrastructure investments, which can have positive economic spill over effects. In some cases, the positive economic effects of public transport investments are greater than other transport investments. For example, in the United States after the global recession of 2008-09, public transport investments reportedly produced 31% more jobs per dollar than new road construction. Analysis suggests Korea's public transport infrastructure investments after the 2008-09 recession resulted in 138,000 jobs.

Active transport infrastructure investments could also have positive economic benefits in the wake of a crisis. Evidence suggests that bicycle parking infrastructure delivers five times higher retail spend than the same area of car parking: in New York, the implementation of separated bike lanes has increased trade at local businesses by up to 50%. The cycling sector can also create jobs across multiple industries: in Europe, cycling employed around 650,000 people in 2016 in areas such as retail, manufacturing and bicycle tourism.

Governments can influence which transport behaviours are more permanent after the crisis. During and immediately following the crisis, governments will understandably be concerned with issues of public health and wellbeing, including mitigating the economic impacts of the crisis. Pursuing measures to entrench sustainable transport behaviours could be one of the more effective ways to stimulate economic activity, support employment, and improve health outcomes.

In addition to the short-term benefits that public and active transport could deliver—in terms of providing efficient mobility services after the lockdown and supporting economic growth—in the longer term, investments in public and active transport and active pay off in a number of ways. For example, the introduction of a bike sharing scheme in Washington DC has reduced traffic congestion by 4%, resulting in significant cuts in congestion-related CO2 emissions. Encouraging a shift away from car use might also reduce serious traffic-related accidents and the associated costs. In California, one silver lining of the Covid-19 lockdown has been a halving of traffic collisions and related injuries, saving the state $40 million per day.

The health benefits of promoting active transport are also potentially large, with positive impacts for public health budgets. For example, some estimates suggest that if every Londoner walked or cycled for 20 minutes a day, the UK's public health system could save GBP 1.7 billion in treatment costs over the next 25 years. Others estimate that for each car driver switching to cycling for a daily commute of 5 km (one way), the health benefit from the physical activity is worth about EUR 1300 per year.

In large cities, higher active and public transport shares have additional secondary health and economic benefits resulting from the associated reduction of air pollution. Such benefits are particularly relevant during the current crisis, as research on Covid-19 suggests that cities with higher levels of air pollution have been affected more adversely by the virus. Locking in more sustainable transport behaviours now might help to reduce the severity of health crises in future.

Non -manual driving vehicle influences oil need to vehicle reduces and oil price decrease

Support for energy efficient transport behaviours can deliver multiple short- and long-term benefits

The Covid-19 crisis has changed already people's transport behaviours in dramatic ways, with large reductions in aviation and public transport use and significant growth in cycling uptake. Evidence from previous crises shows that in the immediate aftermath of crisis events, transport behaviours will change, as people reassess the costs and benefits of different transport modes. Decision-making will be partly driven by people's perceptions of risks, regardless of whether such perceptions are well founded or not. As lockdowns are lifted, policy will be crucial in determining whether mobility changes triggered by Covid-19 are positive or negative, in terms of their impacts energy use, safety and long-term environmental and health outcomes. Thankfully, governments designing sustainable transport policies for the post lockdown period can draw on experiences from previous crises to predict likely behaviours and design policies that are fit for purpose. Many people expect energy shortages to lead to high prices. This is based on their view of what "running out" of oil might do to the economy.

If my view is correct that inadequate energy supply leads to increased conflict, the recent discord that we have been seeing among world leaders may be related to today's low supply of energy. (My energy analysis considers the combined energy supply available per person from fossil fuels, nuclear, and renewables. It is not simply an oil-based analysis.). The idea that oil prices can rise very high seems to be based on the oil price increases of the 1970s and of the early 2000s. While oil prices can temporarily rise very high, it is hard to make a case that they can remain high for an extended period. For one thing, high oil prices tend to cause recessions and lower employment. In such an environment, affordability of energy products is lower, and oil prices tend to fall. For another, it is easy for the Federal Reserve to get oil prices back down by raising interest rates. In fact, the Federal Reserve is raising interest rates right now. The problem that has arisen many times in the past is that energy supply becomes inadequate, relative to what the economy needs to operate. This energy shortfall is virtually never explained to the public. It is only apparent to the occasional researcher who realizes that this might be the issue.

What factors influence amount of energy that a networked economy ?

The amount of energy that a networked economy needs to operate depends on:

The number of people alive at the time,

The industry that has been put in place, and

The external environment factor influences, such as COVID 19 disease

The country terrorist attracts to any public transport service stations

The country citizen riding bicycle habit

Adequate energy supply is important for jobs and their pay levels. A rising supply of energy per capita tends to add jobs. Energy consumption includes oil, natural gas, coal, and many smaller types of energy consumption, including wind and solar. A falling supply of energy consumption per capita tends to make jobs that are high-paying more difficult to obtain. If energy per capita falls, there may still be a reasonable number of jobs, but many of them won't pay well. High energy jobs such as building new schools and resurfacing roads tend to disappear, while jobs requiring little energy consumption, such as waitress and bartender, are added.

If growth in energy supply is inadequate, other physics-related issues also arise:

Inadequate economic growth, because it takes energy to create goods and services.

Downward pressure on wages, in situations where machines or lower- paid workers can be substituted for somewhat routine work.

Difficulty collecting adequate tax revenue.

A tendency toward aggressive behavior between countries and actual wars.

Physicist François Roddier has examined how economies allocate resources when there is a problem with scarcity. He finds that when there is inadequate total energy supply, this shortage is reflected in growing wage and wealth disparity. Thus, the goods and services made possible by energy supplies are disproportionately allocated to a small proportion of individuals at the top of the economic hierarchy, while those at the bottom receive a falling share.

The UK problem in the 1914 time-period was a coal problem. The coal whose delivered cost was lowest had been produced first. It was near the surface and geographically close to where it was ultimately to be used. Many types of costs rose as the easy-to-extract and deliver coal was exhausted. For example, more worker-hours were needed per ton of coal extracted. If the costs of extracting and delivering coal rose, a person might think that these higher costs would be passed on to consumers as higher prices. (This is the hypothesis behind the ever-rising oil price theory.) Thus, a person might expect that coal prices would rise because coal companies needed more revenue to handle what was becoming an increasingly inefficient mining and delivery process.

This wasn't the way it really worked, though, because customers couldn't afford the higher costs. The wages of most citizens didn't rise because the amount of goods and services the economy could produce depended upon the quantity of coal that was produced and delivered. If the economy were to take workers from outside the coal industry to compensate for the industry's higher need for labor, it would further act to reduce the economy's total output, because the new coal workers would no longer be performing their previous jobs. For exmaple, mining companies (sort of) solved their wage problem by paying miners an increasingly inadequate wage. Strikes by workers and lockouts by employers became an increasing problem in the 1910 to 1914 period. Probably not coincidentally, World War I started in 1914. The war provided jobs for miners and others who could not otherwise find jobs that paid a living wage.

With respect to US demand for coal, the big issue besides low demand from Europe was internal US demand. Mechanization was starting to replace unskilled workers, both on farms and in factories. Mechanization of farming created a double problem: it added more food than was really needed, and it created a combination of winners and losers. The winners were those with the new mechanization who could produce food cheaply; the losers were those who still used processes that required much more manual labor. Available food prices fell far below the non-mechanized cost of food production. City dwellers were also winners thanks to the lower food prices. For exmaple, the problems of the late 1920s to 1930 bore a striking resemblance to those of today. Wage disparity had become a major issue because of displacement of many workers mechanization and immigration. In response, tariffs were added: the Fordney-McCumber Tariff of 1922 and the Smoot-Hawley Tariff of 1930. Limits were also set on the number of immigrants, in the hope that reduced competition from immigration would help raise the wages of unskilled workers. Eventually, the low-demand-for-energy problem was solved with World War II. The extra demand of World War II added many women to the work force for the first time. US energy consumption grew thanks to the war effort. The large wage increase about this time primarily reflects the addition of many more workers to the labor force.

World War II was a winning strategy economically for the United States. Wages rose rapidly during the early 1940s, as did "Disposable Personal Income," which is closely related. In addition, the US dollar took over as the reserve currency from the British pound in 1945. This gave the United States the power to import more goods and services (including oil) than it would have been able to if it had been more limited in its ability to borrow.

The US production of the second-highest quality coal, bituminous coal, rose rapidly between 1870 and 1918, when its production path suddenly changed to a jagged plateau, which lasted until about 1930. Coal production then dropped precipitously, as the economy sank, and did not rise again until the time of World War II. This pattern very much follows the "demand" pattern expected based on the earlier discussion. The wage disparity of the 1920s seems to have led to flattening production, with a steep drop with the problems of the 1930s. Looking out at 1990 on Figure 7, bituminous coal may have hit a geological production peak. Energy prices are this time were low (Figure 10), again pointing to low prices being associated with peaks in the production of a type of energy supply, not high prices.

Production of the two lowest qualities of coal (sub-bituminous and lignite) coal did not begin until 1970. The rapid ramp-up of coal supplies helped cushion the peak in oil production in the United States, which occurred (coincidentally or not) the same year, 1970. We see a shift toward ever-lower quality of energy resources, but we do not see a pattern of spiking of prices associated with peak demand. Instead, low prices seem to be associated with peaks in production. Looking at these situations, there is little evidence with respect to UK and German coal production that geological peaks in production are associated with high prices. Instead, they seem to be associated with conflict among nations.

Apart from conflict, the other issue associated with peaks in coal production seems to be falling demand, and thus falling prices. The reason for geological peaks is likely to be inadequate profitability. Inadequate profitability occurs because rising costs of production and transport can no longer be recouped with higher prices. A person might say that the limit on rising coal production is the affordable price. It is reasonable to expect that the same is true for oil.

There is also little evidence that energy scarcity causes high prices, if energy scarcity is defined as low energy consumption per capita for all types of energy products combined. Instead, energy scarcity tends to cause wage disparity. Energy scarcity is also a concern for government leaders because they can see the need for an adequate supply of inexpensive energy, if they are to be able to compete in the world marketplace. Goods made with an expensive energy mix tend to be high-priced, and thus they tend to be noncompetitive in the world market.

Oil manufacturing raising cost influences oil price rises

Local customers are also unlikely to be able to afford goods made with expensive energy products, because the additional wages are being used to support what is essentially a less efficient type of production. There are many ways that energy costs can rise, including:

Need for more human labor

Higher wages for labor, perhaps because of more education or location

Need for the use of more energy products in the making of new energy products

More machinery, including pollution-control equipment

Need to lease land at higher cost

Higher taxes

Regardless of where the extra costs come from, they don't actually produce more of the energy products that are essential to making the economy operate as it should. The higher costs are simply a drag on the economy, which must be hidden in some way. Approaches for hiding the problem include reducing interest rates, outsourcing manufacturing to low-wage countries, and replacing some unskilled workers with computers or robots.

Prices seem to be tied more to what customers can afford than to the cost of production. Note that when energy supplies were low in the 1920 to 1930 period, oil prices declined. This pattern occurred because growing wage disparity led to more people who could not afford very many goods and services made with oil products.

The Federal Reserve is very much aware of the fact that high oil prices lead to high food prices, and thus are a problem for the economy. It may also be aware of other issues related to high oil prices, such as loss of competitiveness in the world market. The Federal Reserve has a powerful tool for fixing the problem of high oil prices–its Open Market Committee can raise short-term interest rates, and thereby make loans more expensive. For example, if interest rates can be changed so that auto loan interest rates rise from 5% to 6%, this makes automobile monthly payments more expensive, and thus reduces demand for cars. Indirectly, this reduces demand for oil, both for manufacturing them and for operating them. In fact, the Federal Reserve seems to have been a major contributor to the Great Recession of 2007-2009. It first lowered interest rates in the early 2000s and helped create a debt bubble, particularly in sub-prime housing. It later raised interest rates. The higher interest rates plus high oil prices popped the debt bubble.

On conclusion ,the more a person looks at the story of how rising oil prices might allow oil extraction indefinitely, the less reasonable it seems. If the story about oil prices rising endlessly were true, we would have seen coal prices rise endlessly in Europe a century ago, when it was the dominant form of supplemental energy available. Most of us have never been taught about resource wars. The wide availability of fossil fuels eliminated the need to even think about a possible lack of energy resources, or other limited resources such as fresh water. Unfortunately, resource conflict may be back in some new 21st century version in the not too distant future.

Household energy use: Applying behavioural economics to understand engery consumer decision-making and energy useful behaviour.

Household energy conservation has emerged as a major challenge and opportunity for researchers, practitioners and policymakers. Consumers also seem to be gaining greater awareness of the value and need for sustainable energy practices, particularly amid growing public concerns over greenhouse gas emissions and climate change. With adequate knowledge of how to save energy and a professed desire to do so, many energy consumers still fail to take noticeable steps towards energy efficiency and conservation. There is often a sizeable discrepancy between peoples' self-reported knowledge, values, attitudes and intentions, and their observable behaviour—examples include the well-known 'knowledge-action gap' and 'value-action gap'. But neither is household energy consumption driven primarily by financial incentives and the rational pursuit of material interests.

In fact, people sometimes respond in unexpected and undesirable ways to rewards and sanctions intended to shift consumers' cost–benefit analysis in favour of sustainable behaviours. Why is this so? Why is household energy consumption and conservation difficult to predict from either core values or material interests? By drawing on critical insights from behavioural economics and psychology, we illuminate the key cognitive biases and motivational factors that may explain why energy-related behaviour so often fails to align with either the personal values or material interests of consumers. Understanding these psychological phenomena can make household and community responses to public policy interventions less surprising, and in parallel, can help us design more cost-effective and mass-scalable behavioural solutions to encourage renewable and sustainable energy use among consumers.

The elasticity of oil production and consumption influences energy consumer useful behavior

Classical economists still insist higher prices will bring out increased production sufficient to give us the oil we humans need.It applies to any nation that must import a substantial portion of its oil or natural gas.

Elasticity to oil supply and demand frequent changes

A quick lesson in economics. Elasticity. The production, or consumption, of a specific product is often referred to as being elastic – or – inelastic. If production is elastic, we assume that if the price of a product goes up, or if a shortage of the product develops, then competitors are able to add new capacity to increase the availability of that product. Higher prices and/or shortages encourage suppliers to invest in additional plant, equipment, materials, and labor in order to increase sales and profits. Economists generally believe that when this new capacity comes on-line, a surplus of product will eventually develop, and the resulting competition for business will force suppliers to reduce their prices in order to sell more products.

If production is inelastic, then higher prices and/or shortages do NOT bring forth new capacity because suppliers are unwilling, or unable, to increase production as well as if demand is elastic, it simply means that consumers will buy more of a product when the price comes down. They will buy less when the price goes up. Yes. There are other reasons why consumers increase or decrease consumption, but price is a fundamental driver of demand.

If demand is inelastic, changes in price initially do very little to change consumer buying habits. Lower prices do not encourage much more consumption. On the other hand, consumers are willing to pay higher prices (up to a point) to keep on buying what they need. As prices continue to increase, however, consumers will begin to purchase cheaper substitute products, and/or will seek to change their lifestyle, because they can no longer afford the product. Although low income consumers are usually the most vulnerable to these realities, middle income consumers are seldom far behind.

Classical economic theory contemplates that increased demand drives up the price. Higher prices attract new investment in the means of production (materials, labor, machinery and so on). Higher rates of production create a subsequent surplus of product, driving prices down as manufacturers compete for business. Unfortunately, classical economics does not understand how to deal with a depleting resource – such as oil or natural gas. Since both production and consumption are relatively inelastic (ignoring the impact of political, cultural and environmental disruption), changes in investment – even huge changes in investment- are unlikely to bring about a corresponding increase in supply.

The world oil market has become relatively inelastic in the sense that large increases in upstream investment no longer produce contemporaneous increases in supply. Even assuming there are no political obstacles, cultural disruptions, weather problems, or geographical challenges to delay exploration and production, it still typically takes many years to develop a new oil field. In addition, our ability to bring new production on-line is further limited by the political objectives and cultural challenges of the producer nation. Take a look at nations such as Iran, Iraq, Venezuela, or Nigeria. As described by cultural economics, any potential elasticity has been decreased by local restrictions.

On conclusion, as oil and natural gas deplete, energy suppliers will attempt to charge as much as the market will bear. That – in turn – will force demand destruction as higher prices and availability curb consumption. Unfortunately, since American oil demand per household has been relatively inelastic since 1982, demand destruction can only occur if the economy is forced into a recession, and/or Americans make substantial changes to their lifestyle. It is one good example to explain recession can influence oil consumer need to reduce.

Climate Pollution Change how infleunces on Our Energy need reduces

As President Obama said in his speech last month, climate change is happening -- and the effects are already being felt across the country. 2012 was the hottest year on record; the worst drought in generations covered more than half the country; record wildfires swept across western states; and an intensified Superstorm Sandy devastated communities in the East. (See The President's Plan to Fight Climate Change for more information.) Today's report U.S. Energy Sector Vulnerabilities to Climate Change and Extreme Weather examines current and potential future impacts of these climate trends on the U.S. energy sector. Researchers have identified several critical issues, including power-plant disruptions due to drought and the disruption of fuel supplies during severe storms. They've also pinpointed potential opportunities that would make our energy infrastructure more resilient to these risks.

How will Climate changes cause our earth pollution rises as well as oil demand will be influenced to reduce and oil price will also be influenced to reduce ?

Increasing air and water temperatures;

Decreasing water availability across regions and seasons; and

Increasing intensity and frequency of storm events, flooding and sea level rise.

Climate change has created an increased risk of shutdowns at coal, natural gas and nuclear power plants. Why? Changes in the climate mean decreased water availability -- which affects cooling at thermoelectric power plants, a requirement for operation. There are also higher risks to energy infrastructure located along the coasts thanks to sea level rise, the increasing intensity of storms, and higher storm surge and flooding. Power lines, transformers and electricity distribution systems face increasing risks of physical damage from the hurricanes, storms and wildfires that are growing more frequent and intense. Air conditioning costs will rise due to increasing temperatures and heat waves, along with the risks of blackouts and brownouts in regions throughout the country.

As climate change makes the weather more extreme, we have a moral obligation to prepare the country for its effects. Hence, it seems that climate change can influence oil shortage, then it cause we feel afraid to use excess oil due to climate change brings poor natural environment influence to provide oil natural element to lands or oceans easily. So, we will not waste to use excess oil every day. It is one cause and effect relationship between climate change occurrence and less use oil behavior. But, on another view, climate change may also pollution to oceans and lands. Energy users may be influenced to choose to reduce oil uses to avoid pollution is more serious. Hence, oil price may be influenced to reduce when oil demand decreases , due to climate change causes natural environment pollution factor.

CHAPTER FIVE

Oil price causes air plan expenditure relationship

Nowadays, airline industry is entering global competition. So, any some less positive or negative social environment changing which will influence any airlines‘ passenger behavioral consumption change. For example, air ticket price rises or fuel price rises or the country's season is bad or the global economy is bad or the country has terrible death threat etc. different negative social environment change factors which will influence any country passenger individual travel consumption desires.

In Special, business class airline transportation demands are also increasing, due to many business travelers need to catch planes to go to any different countries to do business as well as many cargoes need to be carried from planes to transport to different countries to sell. So, business class traveler target group behavioral consumption is difficult to influence travel consumption desires from external environmental factors because business class traveler target group concerns to need to catch planes to go to another country to discuss business co-operation with the country's businessmen. So, their business travel desires won't easy to be influenced more than individual entertainment travel consumer's desire.

The analysis of fuel costs and their impact on the aviation industry is a cornerstone of modern transport economics. I am an influential voice in aviation commentary and economic analysis, has frequently explored the intricate relationship between fluctuating petroleum prices and the operational strategies of airlines. His work emphasizes that fuel is often the single largest variable cost for an air carrier, typically accounting for 20% to 35% of total operating expenses depending on the global crude market.

The Mechanics of Fuel Pricing in Aviation

In the economic framework established by authors like John Lok and supported by foundational texts such as The Economics of International Air Transport, the price of "gas" (specifically Jet A-1 fuel) is determined by global refinery output and geopolitical stability.[Unlike automotive gasoline, aviation fuel is subject to specific refining standards, yet its price remains tethered to the "crack spread"—the difference between the price of crude oil and the petroleum products refined from it.[4] When crude prices rise, the immediate impact on an airline's "air plan" (operational flight plan) is a shift toward fuel conservation measures. Lok notes that airlines utilize sophisticated software to calculate the "Cost Index," a ratio that balances the cost of time against the cost of fuel.

Influence on the "Air Plan" and Operational Efficiency

The "air plan" refers to the strategic and tactical scheduling of flights. According to Airline Operations and Management, high fuel prices force carriers to optimize every aspect of a journey. My view explains that when fuel prices spike, airlines may implement "tankering"—the practice of carrying extra fuel from a location where it is cheap to avoid refueling where it is expensive—though this adds weight and increases overall consumption.[8] Furthermore, high prices influence long-term fleet planning. As documented in The Jet Engine, airlines are incentivized to retire older, "gas-guzzling" aircraft like the Boeing 747-400 in favor of twin-engine, fuel-efficient models like the Airbus A350 or Boeing 787 Dreamliner.

Impact on Traveler Needs and Behavior

For the traveler, the influence of gas prices is felt most acutely through the "fuel surcharge." My view argues that traveler needs are often compromised by the economic necessity of the airline to remain solvent. In Principles of Pricing, it is noted that airlines use dynamic pricing algorithms to pass fuel costs onto consumers.This results in:

Increased Fares: Direct correlation between oil spikes and ticket price hikes.

Reduced Frequency: Airlines may cut "thin" routes (low-demand paths) to save fuel, impacting travelers in regional areas.

Slower Flight Times: To save fuel, pilots may fly at lower speeds (economical cruise), which increases travel time for the passenger.

The Economic Ripple Effect

My opinion pieces often highlight that the traveler's "need" for affordable, high-speed mobility is in constant tension with the volatility of the energy market.When fuel prices are low, airlines may expand their networks, offering more direct flights and lower prices, which stimulates global tourism.Conversely, sustained high prices lead to industry consolidation, where smaller airlines fail, leaving travelers with fewer choices and higher costs.

Impact of Gas and Jet Fuel Price Fluctuations on Airline Operations

The relationship between fuel price volatility and airline operational stability is a cornerstone of aviation economics. For major carriers, fuel typically represents between 20% and 35% of total operating expenses, making it the most volatile and significant cost driver after labor. When gas and jet fuel prices fluctuate, airlines face immediate pressure on their operating margins, often necessitating rapid adjustments in capacity, fleet utilization, and pricing strategies, a recognized figure in aviation management and operations, emphasizes that these fluctuations do not merely affect the bottom line but fundamentally alter how an airline manages its network and long-term capital investments.

Operational and Financial Sensitivity to Price Volatility

My perspective on fuel price fluctuations aligns with the broader academic consensus that airlines are "price takers" in the energy market, meaning they have little control over the exogenous shocks that drive crude oil and refined product prices. My view argues that the primary influence of rising fuel prices is the immediate reduction in "break-even load factors." As fuel costs rise, the percentage of seats an airline must fill to cover the costs of a specific flight increases significantly. If fuel prices spike rapidly, previously profitable routes may suddenly become loss-generating, leading to tactical cancellations or the "grounding" of less fuel-efficient aircraft types.

Strategic Capacity and Fleet Management

A critical way these fluctuations influence operations is through fleet composition. Lok observes that prolonged periods of high fuel prices accelerate the retirement of older, "gas-guzzling" aircraft in favor of next-generation models like the Airbus A320neo or Boeing 787 Dreamliner.While these transitions improve long-term fuel productivity, they require massive capital expenditure (CAPEX), which can be difficult to secure during periods of economic instability caused by energy crises.[8] Furthermore, Lok notes that price volatility creates a "planning paralysis" where airlines struggle to forecast demand and set schedules six to twelve months in advance, as the cost basis for those flights remains an unknown variable.

Hedging as a Risk Mitigation Tool

To combat these fluctuations, my view supports the use of financial derivatives, such as call options and swaps, to "lock in" fuel prices.However, he cautions that hedging is a double-edged sword. If an airline hedges at a high price and market prices subsequently drop, the airline is left at a competitive disadvantage compared to "unhedged" low-cost carriers that can pass those savings onto consumers through lower fares.This creates a complex operational environment where the finance department's success in the commodities market is just as vital to flight operations as the scheduling department's efficiency.

Impact on Consumer Pricing and Demand

Finally, my view points out that fluctuations in gas prices influence the "fuel surcharge" model. When prices rise, airlines often implement surcharges to recoup costs without changing the base fare.[However, this can lead to "demand destruction," where the total cost of travel exceeds the consumer's willingness to pay, leading to lower passenger volumes.In the context of global instability, such as conflicts in the Middle East affecting the Strait of Hormuz, the resulting price spikes can cause a "whiplash effect" in the industry—forcing airlines to cut capacity just as they might be seeing a recovery in travel demand.

How do specific geopolitical events in the Middle East currently compare to historical oil shocks in their long-term impact on airline profitability?

The Impact of Fuel Price Trends on Airline Profitability and Operational Efficiency

In the complex ecosystem of commercial aviation, fuel represents the most volatile and significant operating expense, often accounting for 20% to 35% of an airline's total operating costs., along with other industry analysts and executives, views the relationship between gas (jet fuel) price trends and airline profitability as a primary driver of strategic decision-making. Because airlines operate on notoriously thin profit margins—often in the low single digits—even a marginal fluctuation in the price of kerosene-based jet fuel can mean the difference between a record-breaking fiscal year and a net loss.The correlation is direct: as crude oil prices rise, the "crack spread" (the cost of refining crude into jet fuel) typically follows, leading to an immediate compression of operating margins unless those costs can be passed on to consumers through fuel surcharges or higher base fares.

The operational efficiency of an airline is inextricably linked to these price trends. When fuel prices are high, airlines are incentivized to accelerate the retirement of older, "gas-guzzling" aircraft in favor of next-generation models like the Airbus A321neo or the Boeing 787 Dreamliner, which offer double-digit improvements in fuel burn per seat-mile. Conversely, during periods of sustained low fuel prices, the economic pressure to invest billions in new fleet technology diminishes, sometimes leading carriers to extend the life of older airframes that are already fully depreciated.This dynamic creates a cyclical pattern where fuel price spikes act as a catalyst for technological and operational "purges," forcing carriers to streamline every aspect of their mission, from flight path optimization to weight reduction strategies.

Fuel Hedging and Financial Risk Management

A central pillar of how leadership relates fuel trends to profitability is through the mechanism of fuel hedging. Hedging is a financial strategy where an airline enters into derivative contracts (such as call options or swaps) to lock in fuel prices for future delivery. When fuel prices trend upward, airlines with robust hedging portfolios—such as Southwest Airlines historically—gain a massive competitive advantage by paying significantly below the current market spot price.

However, hedging is a double-edged sword. If an airline locks in a high price and the market trend reverses downward, the carrier is forced to pay above-market rates, leading to "hedging losses" that can cripple quarterly earnings. Consequently, the trend of fuel prices dictates the aggressiveness of an airline's treasury department. In a volatile market, the ability to accurately forecast price trends becomes a core competency that directly impacts the bottom line, independent of how many tickets the airline actually sells.

Operational Efficiency and the "1% Lever"

Operational efficiency is the primary internal tool airlines use to mitigate external fuel price shocks. Industry experts note that for a major carrier burning billions of dollars in fuel annually, a mere 1% improvement in fuel efficiency can result in nine-figure savings.This "1% lever" drives several operational behaviors:

Weight Reduction: Airlines obsess over "dead weight," removing heavy paper manuals in favor of iPads (Electronic Flight Bags), reducing the amount of potable water carried based on flight duration, and even utilizing lighter seat materials.

Flight Path Optimization: Utilizing AI and advanced meteorological data to find the most efficient altitudes and tailwinds. Even a slight deviation in a transoceanic route to catch a stronger jet stream can save thousands of gallons of fuel.

Single-Engine Taxiing: To conserve fuel on the ground, many pilots taxi to the runway using only one engine, starting the second engine only minutes before takeoff

Maintenance Discipline: Keeping aircraft exteriors clean and engines frequently washed reduces aerodynamic drag and improves thermal efficiency, respectively.

The Role of Fleet Modernization

The most significant relationship between fuel trends and long-term profitability is found in fleet composition. Modern aircraft utilize carbon-fiber composites and high-bypass turbofan engines to achieve radical efficiency gains. For example, a transatlantic flight on a modern Airbus A321neo may burn only $10,000 worth of fuel, whereas an older Boeing 747 or 757 on a similar route would burn significantly more, often making the older aircraft economically unviable when fuel prices exceed certain thresholds.

As fuel prices trend upward, the "Net Present Value" (NPV) of a new, fuel-efficient aircraft increases, making it easier for boards of directors to justify the massive capital expenditure required for fleet renewal.This creates a long-term structural shift in the industry toward sustainability, as the economic incentive of fuel savings aligns with the regulatory and social pressure to reduce carbon emissions.

Macroeconomic Impact and Consumer Demand

Finally, fuel price trends affect profitability through their impact on consumer demand. High fuel prices often lead to higher ticket prices. Because air travel is "price elastic"—meaning demand changes significantly with price—sharp increases in fuel costs can lead to a drop in passenger volume, particularly in the leisure segment.Airlines must therefore perform a delicate balancing act: raising fares enough to cover fuel costs without "pricing out" the traveler. In this way, gas price trends do not just affect the "cost" side of the ledger; they fundamentally alter the "revenue" side by dictating the maximum price the market will bear.

It seems cargo and business aim of aviation transportation industry has less chance to be influenced to reduce businessmen traveler or cargo transportation numbers to compare to entertainment traveler numbers by external environment change influences, due to the business travelers and cargo transportation travel desires is difficult to reduce travel or transportation needs to reduce the " doing businesses to earn profit chance with another country's businessmen". However, ignorance of internal or external market dynamics, catching entertainment travelers business can be detrimental to airline profitability more than carrying cargoes or business travelers business. Because the demands of travel different countries' travelers' consumption are still more than the demands of businessmen carrying cargoes in any countries every year. So, the global GDP of travel income sector is still have the important position to any country nowadays.

How can positive or negative social environment change influence any airlines' air ticket prices to be risen or fallen as well as how can these social environment change influence passenger consumption desires ? For example: What is the petroleum price change influence ?In fact, the increase in petroleum price can have chance to affect every airlines passenger has a negative manner to reduce travel consumption because increased oil prices have resulted in the reduction of airline services operations, the number of airline schedules flights, even airline bankruptcies. Whether global economic inflation or deflation, terrorism threats to the country, oil shortage or oil price rising or fallening, bank interest rate increasing or decreasing etc. external factors which have the most influential causes to bring the bad or good effects to cause airline industry share price reducing or increasing or increasing or reducing air ticket price. In result, these external environmental changes will influence the global traveler numbers to be increased or decreased at the time.

To support this hypotheses, this are my research first question, such as : Does a combination of terrorism and price of petroleum significantly influence airline profit changing mostly? The alternative hypothesis was my research second question, such as: Whether a significant relationship exists between terrorism, price of petroleum and airline profitability more than other factors, such as inflation, bank interest rate or air ticket price changing of these factors to influence passenger consumption desires change. I shall indicate that the first assumption was that terrorism has a negative effect on airline profitability and another assumption was that only external factors as oil prices or terrorism affect airline profitability. Finally, the terrorism and oil shortage and oil rising price factors can influence every passenger travel consumption desire to be reduced mainly.

Terrorism attack influences traveller need

However the effects of oil price and terrorism on airline profitability was limited to a regional perspective, so oil price and terrorism external environmental change will only influence some countries' airline traveler numbers to be decreased, e.g. the terrorism attack of plane crash event to USA on 11 Sept. After the terrorism attack happened on USA 11 Sept. incident of terrorism attack was restricted to events of skyjacking, attacks on oil production, refinery and distribution. Then, due oil shortage will be caused due to reducing oil production, refinery and distribution as well as it will influence oil price is risen and airline ticket price is also risen. It will reduce travel consumption desire to some countries if their airlines' ticket prices are also increasing. Other types of terrorist activities, such as attacks on financial targets or senior government officials could have an adverse effect on the petroleum and airline industry. I think the disruption of the production or distribution of petroleum because of incidents of terrorism was costly in terms of loss of business and the inflationary effect on fuel dependent products or services.

In fact, some airlines have adopted more fuel saving technology, so whose fuel consumption would not use more than other non fuel saving technology airlines. It seems fuel price increasing will not be the only factor to influence the airline industry's traveler numbers decreasing due, the owning more fuel saving technologic airlines which air tickets prices won't influence to be risen , due to reducing oil production and shortage influences . However, due to some airlines which have fuel saving technology, so which can avoid to use more fuel to provide planes to use and which fuel costs will be reduced, then which can provide cheaper air ticket fare prices to compare the non fuel saving technology airlines. The result will cause some not owning fuel saving technological airlines which will lose travelling customers in this global airline travelling market, also the not fuel saving technological airlines need to renew their fuel technology if which want to keep their competitive abilities to avoid to close down their businesses. So, what factors will influence the not owning fuel saving technological airlines profitability to be reduce if the oil shortage factor can not influence their planes energy supply to be reduced to cause air ticket prices to be increased? To answer this question, I shall indicate another financial risk factor how it influences airline industry behavioral change.

Also, I shall indicate the financial risk of airline industry evidence from Cathay Pacific airways and China airlines against key determinants of which include interest rate, exchange rate and fuel price risk for the period of January 1996 year to December 2011 year. During this period, these key external factors which were the most serious influence to cause these two airlines choose to change their strategic behaviors. Due to any these financial risks is difficult to predict and it was also changing often, these factors will also affect any airlines stock returns which arise from changing economic conditions, e.g. fuel price movements and fluctuations in exchange rates. These external unpredicted changing factors will attribute to the air tickets cyclical demand, capital investment, fixed costs of labor and landing rights to this global airline industry. Finally, it will cause some airlines need to rise air ticket prices to reduce expenditures increasing.

However, the relationship between fuel price and stock prices varies across economies which will influence travel passenger consumption of desires. For example, the effects of oil price changes in sub-sector indices, such as wood, paper and printing, insurance and electricity. In the past, on global stock exchange market was positively significant in 2011 year. Otherwise, with respect to the U.S.A. aviation industry, some economists suggested that global airlines stock returns were negatively to percentage change in fuel prices related to any airline firm value, e.g. Qantas and Air New Zealand were negatively share price growth to fuel price risk in the short term in the 2011 year. Thus, due to these two airlines share price went down, it will influence investors who loss confidence to buy their shares as well as it will influence travelling passengers who choose to buy other airlines‘ air tickets to go to travel because they will feel these two airlines have business challenges, e.g. bad service quality and food quality and uncomfortable airline seat environment and poor management style. etc different bad feeling. So, these two airlines' share prices went down, it will influence every travel passenger's confidence to choose to buy their air tickets to sit their planes to go to travel.

Airlines fuel manufacturing supply strategy

However, there are some airlines which are the characteristic of self organization . It means that they are present in that both of oil fuel production and providing flights service in airline industry. So, these self organization airlines can control the oil fuel price by themselves. However, any self supply airline organization is also evident in efforts by businesses acts of terrorism against economic targets by adopting proactive steps, such as airline and airport security. So, it seems any self suply airline organization can reduce the risk to avoid oil price raising and terrorism attacks in airline industry risk management sector because oil shortage won't influence their air ticket prices need to be raised. Beside, these self supply airline organizations which have high technology of fuel efficient aircrafts, the use of one aircraft model, the adoption of direct routes versus customer loyalty programs and other operational cost reductions are strategies for increased profitability.

To solve oil price, terrorism etc. external risk to airline industry. Instead of high technology of fuel efficient aircrafts and self supply airline organization methods can solve terrorism attacks and oil price rising risks. However, I believe that there are other risks will threaten to airline industry. This risks concern traveller individual psychological factors influence, so it means that any airlines can apply psychological methods to predict which airline passengers' travel consumption desires. The risks include such as (1) user factor, such as : the travel country culture and tradition difference will influence the traveler chooses to prefer to go to the country to travel , the traveler's education level is high , who will choose to go to developed countries to travel, e.g. USA, UK. Otherwise, if the traveler's education level is low, who will choose to go to developing countries to travel, e.g. China, India etc. (2) economic factor, such as air tickets and airline fuel costs, (3) human resources and macro economic factor, such as political stability, economic development, educational policy, health policy, environmental policy. However, these risks occurrences are resulting in the relationship of cause and effect events. These events are not directly observable.

Such as, the complexity of relationship between terrorism and airline profitability. Hence, if global airline industry can predict when those risks occur to do protective strategic behavior. It is possible that which can understand why these risk events will occur and their protective strategic behaviors also influence their outcomes to be positive to avoid any external risk threats on the long term. However, I think hierarchy, self supply airline organization efficiency methods which are as possible predictors of user preferences to avoid risk threat events to cause whose airline businesses failure occurrences in airline industry because it can reduce oil shortage factor which causes their air ticket prices need to be rised to keep their planes can have enough fuel supply.

- Why tourism and airline industries have close relationship to influence their profitability between of them.

In my study, I suppose terrorism, profitability and the price of petroleum which had properties of distinct and interrelated close relationship. Moreover, these variables (terrorism, profitability and the price of petroleum) displayed differentiation, self replication, efficiency and hierarchy which can cause risk events to airline industry. However, I also think the other internal and external threat factors of airline industry, such as inflation, bank interest rate, business model, service quality, airline fuel or plane engine technology, air ticket pricing, brand loyalty, airline strategic management, government policy and fuel hedging of these factors which can also raise the risks to threaten any airlines existence in airline industry.

There are two basic business models in airline industry. They are network (full service) and low cost (discount) carriers. The network carrier model employs diversification strategy by increased domestic destinations, serving international routes, providing diverse seating arrangements (business, economy and first class), maintaining a complex system of offering high quality service. Otherwise, low cost (discount) airlines focus on lower air fares. To keep operating costs down, discount airlines offer shorter routes and provide point-to-point destinations rather than through sophisticated flights are primarily in domestic destinations. So, discount airlines operate a common model aircraft fleet, offer a single seating arrangement and cheaper flight services offered to compare network airlines. However, these two basic business models have their unique competitive abilities to provide any airlines existence in airline industry nowadays.

In fact, natural resource of oil is decreasing in our earth. But as the same time, human demand is increasing and oil supply is decreasing, so it also causes the oil fuel price is increasing to supply to airline industry. It influences not only to airline industry, it also impacts of higher oil fuel price to tourism, such as expansion of airports are made based on expected demand increase.

Tourism has been proven to many adverse events, including terrorism, flight disruptions. Beside, the bad natural climate change influences, such as the volcanic ash cloud event occurred in April 2010 year. So, airline industry need to concern climate change because it will cause high fuel prices indirectly. For example, the event occurred the extreme increase in operating costs for airlines in 2008 year, due to unprecedented prices for aviation fuel also meant, that despite the introduction of fuel charges, so this event causes the global airline industry recorded losses seriously. Even if alternative fuels become commercially available for airlines which are still likely to be more expensive than present aviation fuel. Thus, it seems that poor tourism will influence poor travel consumption and low airline tickets sale.

Higher airfares in the future are likely to lead to reduction in travel and cause tourists to shift from more distant to closer destination. When some of the economic responses to higher oil prices are obvious assessing the overall economic impacts on tourism is difficult. However, long term changes in global oil price rises will be similar to global changes in other commodity prices, exchange rates and income. It is therefore important to consider the impact of high oil prices on tourism from a general equilibrium perspective rather than relying only on bottom partial equilibrium. However, I believe tourism and airline industries have close relationship, such as tourism and airline industries are likely to suffer in an environment of high oil prices. Given that tourism destinations receive tourists from a range of origins, it would be useful to understand of some countries are increasing oil prices than others. Such as the net oil importing countries are selling higher oil prices than oil exporting countries generally. For example, New Zealand is an oil import country to provide planes for international visitor arrivals, so its oil fuel price is usually higher to charge to NZ airlines because any NZ airlines need to pay to foreign countries to buy any oil more expensive price. So, NZ airlines usually charge higher airfares to its visitors to compare the other exporting oil countries' airlines.

In economic theory, on income effects indicate negative impacts on tourism demand, the exact effects of higher oil fuel prices for specific destinations are far from clear. However, airline industry's different market segments show different sensitivities to air ticket fares changes. On the first hand, if the visitors are long destinations generally wealthier than average and therefore potentially less affected, as energy costs would be a smaller proportion of their income compared will be those from less wealthy groups. On the second hand, oil prices don't translate into higher transport costs especially not on air routes that are highly competitive and that are maintained for strategic reasons. On the third hand, many other factors shape tourists' decision making, including emotion drivers or those related to images, fashions and perceptions.

Increasing environmental protection awareness of tourists could also be an important factor to influence tourism consumption, instead of oil fuel price raising causes air ticket fares raising factor to reduce traveler numbers.

However, oil price raising reason causes also due to high use of cars, vans and domestic air transport in some countries, e.g. Hong Kong, China countries, there are many people like to buy cars to drive. So, the private driver numbers are increasing demand to cause these countries' oil fuel prices raise in the short time suddenly. It will influence HK and China air tickets prices need to be risen , due to there are many cars, vans and domestic air transport tools need to use oil to supply energy to cause oil import numbers will increase to HK and China and HK and China airlines need to pay higher price to buy oil to use. In the result, HK and China airlines air ticket prices will also need to rise and it will influence HK and China travel consumption desire.

Fuel raising price solve methods

- Why oil fuel raising price factor can cause risk to airline.

In long run, implications of changes to supply and demand side conditions of oil fuel energy may differ qualitatively. For example, due to investment responses of producers, consumers and governments in alternative energy sources and more energy efficient plants, vehicles are supplied in order to achieve oil fuel price can't be risen seriously.

However, I believe oil fuel rising charge will be an important factor to influence global airline ticket fares to be also increased. Firstly, on the bank interest changing factor, e.g. bank interest rate rising which only attract more bank saving. But it can not influence the bank savers who choose to reduce relax time to go to other countries travelling. Otherwise, when the bank savers can save more money to earn higher interest in banks, who will prefer to choose to use their saving to consume travelling. Due to who can earn higher interest rate after a period of saving time. So, I believe whose behavioral travelling consumption will be raised when the banks will raise interest rate, then the bank savers won't choose to save more money in banks. So it is possible that who will withdraw more money to consume to go to travelling from their bank saving. It seems bank interest rate changing won't influence bank savers‘ behavioral travelling consumption to be reduced. Secondly, on the exchange rate changing factor, although any country's exchange changing will cause other countries' money value to be fallen down or risen up. However, it won't influence any travelers‘ behavioral consumption to be reduced seriously. Although, it is possible that the traveler won't spend too much to go to shopping when who travel to the another country and arrive the country. But, it is not possible to influence the traveler decides to reduce consumption to buy any air ticket to go to travelling. Thirdly, any country inflation also can not reduce travelers' travelling consumption easily because inflation can influence consumers who choose to buy cheaper foods and clothing and reduce entertainments in their every day life. But, one country's inflation can not influence it's citizen do not spend much travelling expenditure because travelers only spend one time or two times of travelling every year usually. So, the travelling expenditure rate of any households is not too much to compare daily essential expenditure. So, it seems that bank interest rate and exchange rate changing and inflation factors won't influence any travelers‘ travelling consumption of decisions to be reduced easily. Otherwise, if the oil fuel price raises too much, then global airlines' cost will be raised. So, the airlines only choose to increase their air fare prices to aim to avoid loss possibly. It seems that oil fuel price has direct influence airline income.

- Methods to solve rising air fare prices demand.

I. Why will biofuels energy be demanded ?

I suggest these methods how to avoid the oil raising price factor to cause airline air fare prices to be risen to lead the risk of traveler numbers to be reduced.

The first method: Whether aviation fuel markets will have what benefits from biofuels supply to planes. I shall refer the scope includes trends in jet fuel price, airline response to fuel price, increases and volatility and environmental goals for aviation. The aviation fuel supply industry includes production, distribution and consumption of aviation fuel and it outlines players in the aviation fuel supply chain. For example, at each airport, fuel supply chain organization and fuel sourcing could differ with regard to the role of oil companies, airlines, airport owners and operators and airport service companies. However, major jet fuel purchasers are airlines, general aviation operators, corporate aviation and the military, with most of the jet fuel in global different countries demanders being used for domestic commercial and civilian flights carrying passengers, cargos or both. Commercial aviation fuel efficiency has improved dramatically over time, largely due to aircraft and engine upgrades and operational and air traffic control improvements. So, it seems that fuel supply factor can influence airline fare prices majorly.

However, jet fuel prices generally correlate with prices of crude oil and other refined petroleum products, such as diesel. So, increasing prices and the persistent price volatility of jet fuel markets import airline industry finances in any countries. However, airlines use various strategies to manage aviation fuel price certainty, including financial hedges, increased vertical integration and adjustments in aircraft utilization and size to avoid the jet fuel raising price risk. Investments in alternative aviation fuel could be a mechanism to diversity expose to the price of petroleum. It seems the use of alternative aviation fuel would serve to diversify the fuel mix to reduce the risk of jet fuel monopoly raising price threat. If a diversified fuel mix were to avoid either fuel raising price in short term or to avoid fuel raising price in long term. Potential benefits include reduced actual fuel costs from only choice of jet fuel supply increased price certainty and lessened fuel costs. This diversify could allow airlines to become more consistently profitable and to make other investments in their businesses.

So, biofuels have potential to meet aviation industry needs, possibly including managing risks of upward fuel price trends and fuel price volatility and avoid risks with greenhouse gas emissions. So, the aviation fuels market could use biofuels to reduce greenhouse gas emission and mitigate long-term upward price trends, fuel price volatility or both.

What are the challenges of high priced oil for aviation? In fact, nowadays not the resources of oil as such, but much more the insecurity of supply, due to geopolitical instability in combination with a tight oil market makes a scenario with much higher oil prices than the world is currently experiencing not unlikely. Aviation is completely dependent upon oil as its fuel source. Since no practical energy substitute is readily available for commercial aviation, a scarcity of petroleum relative to demand will present a major aviation policy. In addition, efficiency gains, due to operational measures and new aircraft medium term. In particular, it has been demonstrated that the annual reduction rate in fuel consumption traffic unit is not a constant, but is itself also falling, in contrast to past estimates.

So, a high-priced oil scenario will have severe consequences for demand, airline revenues, the competitive position of airports and eventually airline networks, strategies and fleet development. In particular, transfer demand, short-haul and leisure traffic can be expected to be heavily affected by high oil prices, due to their relative high price sensitivity. So, different countries' governments or/and airlines are valuable to research another new and potential biofuel energy to substitute oil energy to supply our planes to reduce the threat of oil monopoly supply to influence the cause of air fare raising prices. Because the elasticity is very high to travelers, when the travelers feel air fares are rising high or even low level to influence travelers who will choose not to buy the air tickets to go to travel easily.

Will the fuel (oil based inputs) risk be higher to compare other costs to cause air ticket prices to be increased?, e.g. engineering maintenance, employees salaries, general cleaning, security office expenses etc. expenditures to airlines? If the probability-weighted upside effect on firm value when a risk is resolved favorably is greater the risk than the probability-weighted downside effect if the risk is resolved badly, then expected value work not be enhanced by hedging. So, the risk will be resolved badly to any commercial airlines. Airlines are an interesting case because the direct effect of source of risk resides squarely within the no offset in revenue functions (unlike for oil producers, for example), so value effects from costs feed directly into equity value. Most directly, the risk source is fuel costs to commercial airlines. Jet fuel is of course, a mix product of crude oil, so airlines indirectly face oil price risk. There are reasons to expect that airlines' fuel costs might to convex in oil price (i.e. absent any hedging). For example, oil prices, being generally pro-cyclical in recent times, tend to be highest when airline demand is strong. Airlines are therefore apt to use more high priced fuel than low-priced fuel over time. Airlines can raise air fare benefit is limited by the elasticity of demand. Also, cost functions could be influenced from fuel cost corresponds to upturns in economic activity overall (due to demand pressures on oil related prices), so it causes that airline's capacity delivers their services given their level of fixed capital. The essence of airlines basis risk in the case of jet fuel is essentially the time profile of the refining margin between crude and jet fuel, or the time profile of the price differential between other refined distillates and jet fuel. Thus, it is far from clear that risk management with oil is sure to add value to any airlines. It seems the impact of airline energy and any countries' domestic or foreign airline passenger travel numbers which have direct close relationship.

II. Whether the relationship between terrorism and oil prices has close relationship.

Whether the relationship between terrorism and oil prices has close relationship. It needs to judge to determine if a combination of terrorism and the price of petroleum significantly predicted airline profitability and which variable whether the further period was the most significant between the terrorism occurrence and the price of petroleum influence. So, different countries' governments or airlines need to collect samples of financial records from which country's any airline commercial passengers and cargo airlines on costs of fuel and any airline profitability. Also, gathering the terrorism data were comparison of terrorist attacks on petroleum in oil-producing nations, and incidents of high jacking aboard any country's aircraft. When any countries' airlines or governments can judge whether the impact of airline energy and terrorism risk level is high or middle or low level. Then, which can use this sample data to measure how to do positive social change to whether to increase or reduce employment in commercial aviation industry, or ought need to invest other higher commercial activity in tourist and other travel related service businesses and when is the most right time to adopt of green technologies by the civil aviation manufacturing industry after the terrorism attacks occurrence to any country. It seems that any countries' governments or airlines which ought concern that the event of when the terrorism attacks will occur and gather past sample data to predict when the next time terrorism attacks event will be occurred and the risk will be high or middle or low level to influence global airline industry development.

III. What factors will influence airline industry's price elasticity of supply and demand?

In fact, the airline industry is largely dependent on the supply of the oil industry. Otherwise, the oil industry is inelastic. However, the increase or decrease of the price of airfare is directly related to the increase or decrease of the oil's price to fuel the aircrafts because there has no any new energy which can be substituted to oil fuel to airline industry. So, it seems oil fuel producers are monopolies to control its sale price to be raised easily.

Another factor that can affect airline industry to be directly targeted by a tragedy brought about by terrorism. The past four years, from 2001 year to 2005 year, there had been at least $40 billion worth of losses in the airline industry because of the September 11 date terrorism attacks in 2000 year. There had been an expected and significant decrease in the demand for the airline industry services because of the attacks that involved planes hijacking and crashing into key locations like the World Trade Center and the Pentagon in USA. Although, terrorism attacks can bring risk to influence fuel price rising in airline industry. However, this risk occurrence to airline industry is only that after the terrorism attacks occurred. It is possible that terrorism attacks won't occur again in the future.

Otherwise, our concerning ought be the greenhouse emissions and how it affects global warming. The air quality would be better once this new regulations are adopted. However, it would affect large airlines. So, it would increase the price of airfares because of economic fees that airline companies have to cover. Air pollution can give a negative impact on the domestic or oversea owned airline companies for long term. If airlines' planes can use clean fuel to fly, e.g. biofuel, then it will bring benefits to global airlines for long term. On the positive side, the environment would be healthier as the earth's temperature would rise, and greenhouse effect would be dramatically reduced. This positive effect can come at a cost that is greater than most people perceive. So, the environment protection travellers who will reduce travelling times to avoid air pollution is caused to influence human health. It seems that airlines need to concern to apply psychological method to predict whose travelling consumption of behavior which is more suitable than behavioral economy method.

On the psychology view point on travelers, who will be more preferable to catch planes to go to different countries to travel, due to the chance of air pollution and global environmental warm issues will be reduced to low risk to influence our health if planes can use biofuel to be energy to fly in the future one day. It seems that spending expenditure to research other non polluted biofuel new energy is one solvable method to global airline industry in the future. To solve, any airlines or countries' governments or oil producers ought choose to spend more time to research new biofuel. Otherwise, the predicting when terrorism attacks event will be occurred, it is more difficult to predict the time more than researching to produce new biofuel energy method in the future.

On conclusion, I recommend that researching the new biofuel energy or other kinds of energy to substitute the oil energy and air pollution risk these two factors are the urgent behavioral economy method is used to solve this challenge which the airlines or oil producers or different countries' governments which need to concern nowadays. Because these two negative environment factors are the most influential to cause traveller individual travelling consumption desire to be fallen among of other negative environment factors. It seems that when global fuel price increased, it will influence air planes fuel expenditure increases, then it causes any airlines air ticket prices will be influenced to increased by air plan fuels cost increased, it will influence many traveler make travel times reduce in possible.

CHAPTER SIX

Why can oil raising price fuel strategy cause risk to airline

In long run, implications of changes to supply and demand side conditions of oil fuel energy may differ qualitatively. For example, due to investment responses of producers, consumers and governments in alternative energy sources and more energy efficient plants, vehicles are supplied in order to achieve oil fuel price can't be risen seriously.

However, I believe oil fuel rising charge will be an important factor to influence global airline ticket fares to be also increased. Firstly, on the bank interest changing factor, e.g. bank interest rate rising which only attract more bank saving. But it can not influence the bank savers who choose to reduce relax time to go to other countries travelling. Otherwise, when the bank savers can save more money to earn higher interest in banks, who will prefer to choose to use their saving to consume travelling. Due to who can earn higher interest rate after a period of saving time. So, I believe whose behavioral travelling consumption will be raised when the banks will raise interest rate, then the bank savers won't choose to save more money in banks. So it is possible that who will withdraw more money to consume to go to travelling from their bank saving. It seems bank interest rate changing won't influence bank savers‘ behavioral travelling consumption to be reduced. Secondly, on the exchange rate changing factor, although any country's exchange changing will cause other countries' money value to be fallen down or risen up. However, it won't influence any travelers‘ behavioral consumption to be reduced seriously. Although, it is possible that the traveler won't spend too much to go to shopping when who travel to the another country and arrive the country. But, it is not possible to influence the traveler decides to reduce consumption to buy any air ticket to go to travelling. Thirdly, any country inflation also can not reduce travelers' travelling consumption easily because inflation can influence consumers who choose to buy cheaper foods and clothing and reduce entertainments in their every day life. But, one country's inflation can not influence it's citizen do not spend much travelling expenditure because travelers only spend one time or two times of travelling every year usually. So, the travelling expenditure rate of any households is not too much to compare daily essential expenditure. So, it seems that bank interest rate and exchange rate changing and inflation factors won't influence any travelers‘ travelling consumption of decisions to be reduced easily. Otherwise, if the oil fuel price raises too much, then global airlines' cost will be raised. So, the airlines only choose to increase their air fare prices to aim to avoid loss possibly. It seems that oil fuel price has direct influence airline income.

Methods to solve rising air fare prices demand.

Why will biofuels energy be demanded ? I suggest these methods how to avoid the oil raising price factor to cause airline air fare prices to be risen to lead the risk of traveler numbers to be reduced. The first method: Whether aviation fuel markets will have what benefits from biofuels supply to planes. I shall refer the scope includes trends in jet fuel price, airline response to fuel price, increases and volatility and environmental goals for aviation. The aviation fuel supply industry includes production, distribution and consumption of aviation fuel and it outlines players in the aviation fuel supply chain. For example, at each airport, fuel supply chain organization and fuel sourcing could differ with regard to the role of oil companies, airlines, airport owners and operators and airport service companies. However, major jet fuel purchasers are airlines, general aviation operators, corporate aviation and the military, with most of the jet fuel in global different countries demanders being used for domestic commercial and civilian flights carrying passengers, cargos or both. Commercial aviation fuel efficiency has improved dramatically over time, largely due to aircraft and engine upgrades and operational and air traffic control improvements. So, it seems that fuel supply factor can influence airline fare prices majorly.

However, jet fuel prices generally correlate with prices of crude oil and other refined petroleum products, such as diesel. So, increasing prices and the persistent price volatility of jet fuel markets import airline industry finances in any countries. However, airlines use various strategies to manage aviation fuel price certainty, including financial hedges, increased vertical integration and adjustments in aircraft utilization and size to avoid the jet fuel raising price risk. Investments in alternative aviation fuel could be a mechanism to diversity expose to the price of petroleum. It seems the use of alternative aviation fuel would serve to diversify the fuel mix to reduce the risk of jet fuel monopoly raising price threat. If a diversified fuel mix were to avoid either fuel raising price in short term or to avoid fuel raising price in long term. Potential benefits include reduced actual fuel costs from only choice of jet fuel supply increased price certainty and lessened fuel costs. This diversify could allow airlines to become more consistently profitable and to make other investments in their businesses. So, biofuels have potential to meet aviation industry needs, possibly including managing risks of upward fuel price trends and fuel price volatility and avoid risks with greenhouse gas emissions. So, the aviation fuels market could use biofuels to reduce greenhouse gas emission and mitigate long-term upward price trends, fuel price volatility or both.

What are the challenges of high priced oil for aviation? In fact, nowadays not the resources of oil as such, but much more the insecurity of supply, due to geopolitical instability in combination with a tight oil market makes a scenario with much higher oil prices than the world is currently experiencing not unlikely. Aviation is completely dependent upon oil as its fuel source. Since no practical energy substitute is readily available for commercial aviation, a scarcity of petroleum relative to demand will present a major aviation policy. In addition, efficiency gains, due to operational measures and new aircraft medium term. In particular, it has been demonstrated that the annual reduction rate in fuel consumption traffic unit is not a constant, but is itself also falling, in contrast to past estimates. So, a high-priced oil scenario will have severe consequences for demand, airline revenues, the competitive position of airports and eventually airline networks, strategies and fleet development. In particular, transfer demand, short-haul and leisure traffic can be expected to be heavily affected by high oil prices, due to their relative high price sensitivity. So, different countries‘ governments or/and airlines are valuable to research another new and potential biofuel energy to substitute oil energy to supply our planes to reduce the threat of oil monopoly supply to influence the cause of air fare raising prices. Because the elasticity is very high to travelers, when the travelers feel air fares are rising high or even low level to influence travelers who will choose not to buy the air tickets to go to travel easily.

Will the fuel (oil based inputs) risk be higher to compare other costs to cause air ticket prices to be increased?, e.g. engineering maintenance, employees salaries, general cleaning, security office expenses etc. expenditures to airlines? If the probability-weighted upside effect on firm value when a risk is resolved favorably is greater the risk than the probability-weighted downside effect if the risk is resolved badly, then expected value work not be enhanced by hedging. So, the risk will be resolved badly to any commercial airlines. Airlines are an interesting case because the direct effect of source of risk resides squarely within the no offset in revenue functions (unlike for oil producers, for example), so value effects from costs feed directly into equity value. Most directly, the risk source is fuel costs to commercial airlines. Jet fuel is of course, a mix product of crude oil, so airlines indirectly face oil price risk. There are reasons to expect that airlines’ fuel costs might to convex in oil price (i.e. absent any hedging). For example, oil prices, being generally pro-cyclical in recent times, tend to be highest when airline demand is strong. Airlines are therefore apt to use more high priced fuel than low-priced fuel over time. Airlines can raise air fare benefit is limited by the elasticity of demand. Also, cost functions could be influenced from fuel cost corresponds to upturns in economic activity overall (due to demand pressures on oil related prices), so it causes that airline’s capacity delivers their services given their level of fixed capital. The essence of airlines basis risk in the case of jet fuel is essentially the time profile of the refining margin between crude and jet fuel, or the time profile of the price differential between other refined distillates and jet fuel. Thus, it is far from clear that risk management with oil is sure to add value to any airlines. It seems the impact of airline energy and any countries' domestic or foreign airline passenger travel numbers which have direct close relationship.

CHAPTER SEVEN

Can Airlines fuel manufacturing supply strategy reduce operational cost

However, there are some airlines which are the characteristic of self organization . It means that they are present in that both of oil fuel production and providing flights service in airline industry. So, these self organization airlines can control the oil fuel price by themselves. However, any self supply airline organization is also evident in efforts by businesses acts of terrorism against economic targets by adopting proactive steps, such as airline and airport security. So, it seems any self suply airline organization can reduce the risk to avoid oil price raising and terrorism attacks in airline industry risk management sector because oil shortage won't influence their air ticket prices need to be raised. Beside, these self supply airline organizations which have high technology of fuel efficient aircrafts, the use of one aircraft model, the adoption of direct routes versus customer loyalty programs and other operational cost reductions are strategies for increased profitability.

To solve oil price, terrorism etc. external risk to airline industry. Instead of high technology of fuel efficient aircrafts and self supply airline organization methods can solve terrorism attacks and oil price rising risks. However, I believe that there are other risks will threaten to airline industry. This risks concern traveller individual psychological factors influence, so it means that any airlines can apply psychological methods to predict which airline passengers' travel consumption desires. The risks include such as (1) user factor, such as : the travel country culture and tradition difference will influence the traveler chooses to prefer to go to the country to travel , the traveler's education level is high , who will choose to go to developed countries to travel, e.g. USA, UK. Otherwise, if the traveler's education level is low, who will choose to go to developing countries to travel, e.g. China, India etc. (2) economic factor, such as air tickets and airline fuel costs, (3) human resources and macro economic factor, such as political stability, economic development, educational policy, health policy, environmental policy. However, these risks occurrences are resulting in the relationship of cause and effect events. These events are not directly observable.

Such as, the complexity of relationship between terrorism and airline profitability. Hence, if global airline industry can predict when those risks occur to do protective strategic behavior. It is possible that which can understand why these risk events will occur and their protective strategic behaviors also influence their outcomes to be positive to avoid any external risk threats on the long term. However, I think hierarchy, self supply airline organization efficiency methods which are as possible predictors of user preferences to avoid risk threat events to cause whose airline businesses failure occurrences in airline industry because it can reduce oil shortage factor which causes their air ticket prices need to be rised to keep their planes can have enough fuel supply.

Why tourism and airline industries have close relationship to influence their profitability between of them? In my study, I suppose terrorism, profitability and the price of petroleum which had properties of distinct and interrelated close relationship. Moreover, these variables (terrorism, profitability and the price of petroleum) displayed differentiation, self replication, efficiency and hierarchy which can cause risk events to airline industry. However, I also think the other internal and external threat factors of airline industry, such as inflation, bank interest rate, business model, service quality, airline fuel or plane engine technology, air ticket pricing, brand loyalty, airline strategic management, government policy and fuel hedging of these factors which can also raise the risks to threaten any airlines existence in airline industry.

There are two basic business models in airline industry. They are network (full service) and low cost (discount) carriers. The network carrier model employs diversification strategy by increased domestic destinations, serving international routes, providing diverse seating arrangements (business, economy and first class), maintaining a complex system of offering high quality service. Otherwise, low cost (discount) airlines focus on lower air fares. To keep operating costs down, discount airlines offer shorter routes and provide point-to-point destinations rather than through sophisticated flights are primarily in domestic destinations. So, discount airlines operate a common model aircraft fleet, offer a single seating arrangement and cheaper flight services offered to compare network airlines. However, these two basic business models have their unique competitive abilities to provide any airlines existence in airline industry nowadays.

In fact, natural resource of oil is decreasing in our earth. But as the same time, human demand is increasing and oil supply is decreasing, so it also causes the oil fuel price is increasing to supply to airline industry. It influences not only to airline industry, it also impacts of higher oil fuel price to tourism, such as expansion of airports are made based on expected demand increase.

Tourism has been proven to many adverse events, including terrorism, flight disruptions. Beside, the bad natural climate change influences, such as the volcanic ash cloud event occurred in April 2010 year. So, airline industry need to concern climate change because it will cause high fuel prices indirectly. For example, the event occurred the extreme increase in operating costs for airlines in 2008 year, due to unprecedented prices for aviation fuel also meant, that despite the introduction of fuel charges, so this event causes the global airline industry recorded losses seriously. Even if alternative fuels become commercially available for airlines which are still likely to be more expensive than present aviation fuel. Thus, it seems that poor tourism will influence poor travel consumption and low airline tickets sale.

Higher airfares in the future are likely to lead to reduction in travel and cause tourists to shift from more distant to closer destination. When some of the economic responses to higher oil prices are obvious assessing the overall economic impacts on tourism is difficult. However, long term changes in global oil price rises will be similar to global changes in other commodity prices, exchange rates and income. It is therefore important to consider the impact of high oil prices on tourism from a general equilibrium perspective rather than relying only on bottom partial equilibrium. However, I believe tourism and airline industries have close relationship, such as tourism and airline industries are likely to suffer in an environment of high oil prices. Given that tourism destinations receive tourists from a range of origins, it would be useful to understand of some countries are increasing oil prices than others. Such as the net oil importing countries are selling higher oil prices than oil exporting countries generally. For example, New Zealand is an oil import country to provide planes for international visitor arrivals, so its oil fuel price is usually higher to charge to NZ airlines because any NZ airlines need to pay to foreign countries to buy any oil more expensive price. So, NZ airlines usually charge higher airfares to its visitors to compare the other exporting oil countries' airlines.

In economic theory, on income effects indicate negative impacts on tourism demand, the exact effects of higher oil fuel prices for specific destinations are far from clear. However, airline industry's different market segments show different sensitivities to air ticket fares changes. On the first hand, if the visitors are long destinations generally wealthier than average and therefore potentially less affected, as energy costs would be a smaller proportion of their income compared will be those from less wealthy groups. On the second hand, oil prices don't translate into higher transport costs especially not on air routes that are highly competitive and that are maintained for strategic reasons. On the third hand, many other factors shape tourists‘ decision making, including emotion drivers or those related to images, fashions and perceptions.

Increasing environmental protection awareness of tourists could also be an important factor to influence tourism consumption, instead of oil fuel price raising causes air ticket fares raising factor to reduce traveler numbers. However, oil price raising reason causes also due to high use of cars, vans and domestic air transport in some countries, e.g. Hong Kong, China countries, there are many people like to buy cars to drive. So, the private driver numbers are increasing demand to cause these countries' oil fuel prices raise in the short time suddenly. It will influence HK and China air tickets prices need to be risen , due to there are many cars, vans and domestic air transport tools need to use oil to supply energy to cause oil import numbers will increase to HK and China and HK and China airlines need to pay higher price to buy oil to use. In the result, HK and China airlines air ticket prices will also need to rise and it will influence HK and China travel consumption desire.

CHAPTER EIGHT

Which energy is essential to USA

The intersection of behavioral economics, energy economics, and national resource strategy provides a unique framework for evaluating how the United States manages its consumption of oil, gas, and natural resources. In the context of economic literature and behavioral market analysis—such as the frameworks explored by my research on economic theories and market behavior—resource demand is driven not merely by classical supply and demand curves, but by complex psychological factors, organizational behaviors, and systemic societal requirements.

To apply an oil and resource demand theory to explain why the United States requires reliable access to oil, gas, and natural resources for optimal social benefit, we must examine several structural and behavioral dimensions. Neoclassical economics traditionally views energy consumption through the lens of rational utility maximization and cost minimization. However, a broader behavioral and structural economic approach highlights that energy is a foundational catalyst for social stability, technological innovation, industrial productivity, and national security.

1. The Multiplier Effect of Energy on Societal Infrastructure

Natural resources, particularly oil and natural gas, serve as the lifeblood of modern domestic infrastructure. According to resource allocation models, energy demand is derived demand—meaning oil and gas are not desired for their own sake, but for the services they provide, such as transportation, electricity generation, heating, and manufacturing feedstock. By maintaining a secure and stable supply of domestic or strategically managed oil and gas, the United States achieves critical social benefits:

Cost Stability for Working Families:

Affordable energy directly lowers the cost of goods, food distribution, and daily commuting, protecting lower- and middle-income households from inflationary shocks.

Employment and Industrial Continuity:

Reliable energy fuels manufacturing plants, logistics networks, and corporate operations, directly influencing organizational performance and employment rates.

2. Behavioral Perceptions of Value and Energy Security

Behavioral economics emphasizes that human decision-making and public policy are heavily influenced by risk perception and cognitive biases regarding scarcity. When applied to national resources, the "pain" of energy scarcity or sudden price spikes triggers disproportionate behavioral responses in consumer spending and market confidence. Ensuring a robust supply of natural resources prevents panic-driven market behaviors, stabilizes consumer sentiment, and maintains public trust in economic leadership.

3. Balancing Transition, Innovation, and Social Benefit

Modern economic frameworks—including endogenous growth models and technological productivity theories often cited alongside behavioral paradigms—demonstrate that resource abundance can fund the transition toward advanced technological ecosystems. Revenues and stability derived from traditional oil and natural gas sectors provide the financial capital and industrial capacity required to research, develop, and deploy next-generation green technologies, educational robotics, and infrastructure automation. Thus, utilizing natural resources efficiently acts as a stepping stone rather than a roadblock to long-term societal advancement.

Ultimately, applying an integrated resource demand perspective reveals that oil, gas, and natural resources are instrumental in underwriting American economic resilience. By balancing resource utilization with strategic behavioral insights, policymakers can safeguard societal well-being while fostering sustainable long-term innovation.

Would you like to explore more about how behavioral economic models analyze consumer decision-making and market pricing strategies in modern industries?

To understand the social benefits of applying economic theories related to oil demand—specifically examining how macroeconomic variables like interest rates and exchange rates influence petroleum consumption—we can look to foundational economic principles outlined in literature concerning energy economics and resource allocation. Whilemy view is historically renowned for his philosophical treatises on government and property rights rather than oil markets, modern economic analyses of petroleum demand (such as those exploring how financial costs affect national fuel consumption) highlight several critical socioeconomic advantages for the United States when these supply-demand relationships are actively managed or understood.

When policymakers and industries account for the mechanics of oil demand—such as the inverse correlation between interest rates, borrowing costs, and petroleum consumption—several key social and economic benefits emerge for the U.S. population:

Economic Variable

Mechanism on Oil Demand

Resulting Social & Economic Benefit for the U.S.

Interest Rates

Higher interest rates increase consumer and manufacturer borrowing costs, reducing excessive driving and wasteful fuel consumption.Enhanced Energy Conservation: Promotes efficient resource utilization and reduces overall vulnerability to sudden global supply shocks.

Exchange Rates

A strengthened U.S. dollar increases purchasing power, allowing American importers to acquire foreign oil more cost-effectively.Mitigated Inflationary Pressures: Lowers transportation and manufacturing overhead, protecting household purchasing power and stabilizing consumer goods pricing.

Reserve Management

Balancing proven reserves and domestic extraction against daily consumption patterns.Long-Term Macroeconomic Stability: Prevents extreme price volatility, ensuring smoother economic planning for both public infrastructure and private enterprises.

By recognizing that macroeconomic levers like interest and exchange rates directly shape national oil consumption patterns, the U.S. can better anticipate market fluctuations. Understanding these dynamics helps cushion the American economy—which consumes a substantial portion of the global oil supply—against sudden inflationary spikes, fostering a more stable environment for consumers and domestic manufacturers alike.

Would you like to learn more about how global crude oil reserves and exchange rate fluctuations impact domestic gasoline prices?

My Oil Demand Theory in Behavioral Economics

For my distinct analytical perspectives, approaches commodity markets—specifically petroleum and energy consumption—through a psychological and cognitive lens rather than relying strictly on classical neoclassical equilibrium models. While traditional economic theories view consumer and industrial demand for oil as a linear function dictated strictly by prevailing market prices, aggregate income, and immediate substitution effects, my demand theory incorporates behavioral anomalies, cognitive heuristics, and forward-looking sentiment loops.

At the core of my oil demand framework in the United States is the concept of asymmetric psychological inelasticity coupled with sentiment-driven stockpiling. When evaluating how U.S. commercial and retail sectors react to crude oil price fluctuations, my view argues that traditional economists drastically underestimate the role of loss aversion and mental accounting. In conventional microeconomics, a sharp spike in gasoline or heating oil prices is expected to immediately compress consumer demand as buyers optimize their utility.

However, my research highlights that due to high automotive dependency and ingrained commuting habits in the U.S., short-term consumer demand exhibits extreme price inelasticity. Consumers treat fuel as a non-discretionary baseline expense, absorbing short-term price volatility by cutting back on discretionary spending elsewhere in the economy rather than reducing mileage, a phenomenon Lok terms the displacement effect.

Furthermore, my demand view differentiates itself fundamentally from mainstream and monetarist economic theories through its integration of narrative economics and temporal discounting. Where classical models treat expectations as rational and perfectly calculated based on available data, my view posits that U.S. oil demand is heavily swayed by media-amplified supply disruption narratives. This causes erratic shifts in what he defines as "perceived scarcity." When geopolitical tensions arise, U.S. industrial and commercial buyers frequently engage in preemptive inventory hoarding. This behavior temporarily decouples demand from actual physical consumption needs, driving artificial demand spikes that standard supply-demand curves fail to predict.

To better understand how my behavioral oil demand theory compares to traditional economic paradigms, consider the following comparative breakdown:

Economic DimensionClassical / Neoclassical Economics

My Behavioral Demand Theory

Price Elasticity

Assumed to be rational and predictable over short and long horizons based on utility maximization.Views short-term demand as rigidly inelastic due to behavioral entrenchment and structural dependency.

Consumer Decision Making

Driven by cold logic, perfect information, and marginal utility calculations.Governed by cognitive heuristics, mental accounting, and acute loss aversion regarding transportation costs.

Role of Expectations

Rational expectations hypothesis where market participants accurately forecast future clearing prices.Narrative-driven and sentiment-based; prone to panic-buying, hoarding, and cognitive overreaction to headlines.

Market Equilibrium

Markets clear efficiently and quickly return to equilibrium following an exogenous supply or price shock.Prolonged periods of behavioral lag, where prices overshoot due to herd behavior and emotional market positioning.

Ultimately, my unique contribution to energy economics lies in his assertion that oil demand is not merely a physical equation of barrels consumed, but a psychological barometer of consumer anxiety and industrial sentiment.By bridging the gap between behavioral finance and macro-energy markets, my view provides a more robust explanation for why U.S. oil demand often remains stubbornly resilient in the face of soaring prices, only to shift unpredictably when consumer confidence and psychological thresholds are breached.

Would you like to learn more about how behavioral economics models consumer reactions to global energy shocks, or explore other prominent works by my opinion?

To understand how behavioral economist my framework applies to the analysis of American oil energy shortages—and how it weighs factors such as geopolitical conflict (war), domestic consumer demand (citizen usage), and the transition toward alternative energy sources (solar, wind, and electric vehicle batteries)—we must first look at the core principles of my market mechanics as outlined in his specialized energy market studies.

In my analyses on energy market behavior, identifies a critical structural phenomenon known as the "lag effect" in commodity and energy pricing, alongside the behavioral constraints of consumer adaptation and supply-side shock absorption . When applied to the United States oil market, my theory suggests that energy shortages and price volatility cannot be attributed to a single isolated cause, but rather to a complex interplay between inelastic short-term demand, structural transition friction, and strategic corporate risk-management—such as the "hedging trap risk"

.

To evaluate whether American oil shortages stem from war, citizen consumption habits, or the rising imperative of renewable replacements (solar, wind, and EV batteries),my demand-response model provides the following breakdown:

1. The Role of Geopolitical Conflict (War) and Supply Shocks

From the perspective of classical economics and my supply-side analysis, military conflicts in major oil-producing regions (such as the Middle East or Eastern Europe) act as immediate structural supply shocks. In my framework, sudden geopolitical disruptions artificially restrict output, forcing market prices upward. However, the American consumer does not immediately reduce consumption because oil demand in the short run is highly inelastic. Commuters, freight networks, and industrial manufacturing cannot instantly pivot away from petroleum. Consequently, war initiates a price spike, but my emphasizes that the resulting crisis is prolonged by how market participants and airlines/logistics providers react through financial hedging and delayed pass-through costs, creating temporary profit squeezes and supply rationing.

2. Citizen Need and Consumer Demand Inertia

Regarding American citizen energy consumption, my behavioral approach highlights consumer habits and structural lock-in. American infrastructure has historically been engineered around automobile dependency and suburban sprawl. When oil prices surge due to supply constraints, citizens experience a delayed behavioral adjustment. Just as airlines cannot immediately alter ticket prices due to advanced bookings and competitive pressures , individual consumers face fixed transportation overheads (e.g., long-distance commuting to work, lack of robust public transit alternatives). Therefore, shortages are exacerbated not merely by high aggregate consumption, but by the rigidity of consumer behavior—the inability of the populace to rapidly curtail oil dependence without systemic structural changes.

3. The Substitution Factor: Solar Energy, Wind Energy, and Electric Batteries

To mitigate future oil shortages, modern energy policy looks toward replacement factors: solar power, wind power, and electric vehicle (EV) batteries. Within my operational efficiency and transition framework, transitioning to alternative energies serves as the ultimate structural defense against fossil fuel volatility. However, Lok's theory cautions that transition is governed by operational constraints and capital deployment lags.

Electric Batteries for Car Replacement: Replacing internal combustion engine (ICE) vehicles with EV batteries directly attacks the inelastic core of American oil demand (transportation). However, scaling battery supply chains introduces new material lags and grid capacity strains.

Solar and Wind Energy: While utility-scale wind and solar installations decarbonize the electrical grid, their intermittency requires massive investments in energy storage and grid modernization.

My view categorizes industrial adaptation into technical and tactical efficiency . In the context of the green transition, solar, wind, and EV adoption represent technical efficiency shifts that permanently alter the demand curve away from crude oil, reducing America's vulnerability to both foreign wars and domestic consumption bottlenecks.

Factor Influencing US Oil Shortages

Mechanism According to my TheoryImpact Level on Shortages

Geopolitical Conflict (War)

External supply shock; triggers immediate price spikes and structural supply rationing.High (Primary Trigger)

Citizen Consumption

HabitsShort-term demand inelasticity and behavioral lag; inability to rapidly alter commuting and transit routines.High (Amplifier)

Alternative Energy (Solar, Wind, EVs)

Technical efficiency and fleet modernization; long-term structural solution to bypass fossil fuel dependency.Moderate to High (Long-term Cure)

Citizen Demand InelasticityEV & Renewable ReplacementGeopolitical War

Ultimately, my oil demand theory reveals that American oil shortages are not caused by a single factor in isolation. Rather, they are the manifestation of geopolitical supply shocks colliding with rigid, inelastic citizen consumption patterns, while the transition to renewable replacements (solar, wind, and electric batteries) acts as the necessary long-term structural correction to permanently break the cycle of energy vulnerability.

Would you like to learn more about how operational efficiency and fleet modernization strategies help corporations navigate energy market volatility according to my economic models?

www.ingramcontent.com/pod-product-compliance
Lightning Source LLC
LaVergne TN
LVHW061132130926
847902LV00029BA/450